S0-ABB-136

INSPIRATIONAL
GRAVITY

INSPIRATIONAL GRAVITY

Grounding the Life that Inspires You

Ted Case

CASE DYNAMICS, INC.
GOLDEN, COLORADO

Inspirational Gravity
Copyright © 2007 by Ted Case. All rights reserved.

This book may not be reproduced, in whole or in part, including illustrations, in any
form (beyond that copying permitted by Sections 107 and 108 of the U. S. Copyright
Law and except by reviewers for the public press), without written permission from the
publisher.

Requests for information should be addressed to:
Case Dynamics, Inc.
1150 Golden Circle, Unit 202
Golden, CO 80401

ISBN-13: 978-0-9793707-0-0
ISBN-10: 09793707-0-1

Edited by Maude Adjarian
Cover Design & Graphics by Kurt Augustin Design

Printed in the United States of America.

FOR ROSE

CONTENTS

ACKNOWLEDGMENTS

This book took a lot of experiences to write. Some of those experiences could almost be thought of as my own but the vast majority clearly involved other people. It is easy to make the argument that the book was co-created in everyway. So, many thanks to all those who have shared in experiences that have contributed to the writing of this book.

Thanks in particular to:

Rose who always supported my ideas and dreams. Also, thanks to my daughters Kristi, Abby, Julie, and Tiffany who, I think, have wondered more than once whether this was a phantom book that would never actually see the light of day. I thank them for giving to me as much encouragement and optimism as I hope I have given them.

A significant part of this book is about learning and I have gotten plenty of that from mentors like Joey Hubbard, Patricia Heyman, and Martha Boston. Thanks to them for their special insight and understanding, which has helped me to formulate many of the ideas in this book. Many thanks to Maude Adjarian for her wonderful editing skills and her ability to make the book better without changing my ideas. Thanks also to Kurt Augustin for the wonderful graphics that help bring the book to life.

Finally, I am grateful to all those who have been clients and seminar participants for their interest and personal desire to grow and prosper. I am quite sure that as teacher/facilitator, I often learned more than they did in our experiences together.

1

2

INTRODUCTION

You cannot teach a man anything.
You can only help him discover it within himself.
                                                            Galileo

The idea of *grounding the life that inspires you* might seem like a paradox. How can inspiration and grounding take place in the same time and space? Grounding suggests hard facts and reality while inspiration suggests fantasy and imagination. These concepts don't seem to get along very well together. Indeed, when you take a person who is very grounded and put him or her with someone who is very imaginative and inspired you might find they have some challenges working together.

Have you ever struggled between an idea that inspires you and the reality of your current situation? You might have a great idea for a business and at the same time be thinking about your current demands where family, finances and so forth are concerned. Those practical demands sometimes don't fit well with your inspiration.

Although grounding and inspiration often don't seem to coexist well in the present moment, they can work very well in different times and spaces. In other words, if I allow myself to be inspired now by opening up to imagination and fantasy and then later ground those ideas by taking action in the best way possible, then that partnership can be magical. In more present-day terms, it can be transformative.

This book is about transformation and specifically; how you can support the changes you want in your life. *Webster's Encyclopedic Unabridged Dictionary* defines the word "transform" in this way: "to change in form, appearance, or structure; metamorphose." In practical terms, that can mean changing from not having a business to building one. It can mean changing from being physically unhealthy, to being healthy. And it can mean changing from not having a significant other in your life to manifesting the relationship you want.

Dr. Wayne Dyer is a teacher of transformational wisdom and the power of intention. He, along with others like Eckhart Tolle (*The Power of Now*) and Shakti Gawain (*Creative Visualization*), talk about co-creating with "source." That creative intention is very much about bringing change into one's life.

Their discussions are on target when they talk about that creative intention and how we can support it by being clear in our inspired ideas and adding momentum to those ideas through intention. There is more, however. And the more that occurs cannot exist in the same time and space as those creative ideas and visualization. Manifestation of your inspired ideas is a process of becoming, which includes grounding. It is not just a state of intention. There is the need for action and there is the need for new learning in order for that change to be ongoing. And there is the need for a way to integrate those three things.

The good news is that you don't have to learn how to be inspired or how to take action. Nor do you need to learn how to learn in order to discover those new ideas. They are parts of the natural process that is your experience. In other words, manifesting change that is fulfilling is your nature not your goal. Consider the alchemists of the Middle Ages and Renaissance periods in history. The alchemists devoted their lives to searching for the magical process that would change lead to gold and to finding an elixir for eternal life. What they didn't realize was that the real power they sought was an integral part of their own experience of who they were. In other words, that magical process or transformative ability is a natural gift not an external characteristic of one material or another.

Suppose, for example, that one day you find yourself watching a beautiful sunset with your dog sitting next to you sharing the experience. You are amazed at the incredible colors of the sky and clouds and your sense of beauty and vastness is almost overwhelming. You turn to your dog and say, "wow, that was amazing!" Your dog looks at you apparently oblivious to the sunset and waits expectantly for you to do something.

You might ask yourself, did my dog or I have the deeper experience? In other words, who had and has the greater capacity for experience? This question is very important because it locates value, which is the gift.

The sunset has no inherent value regardless of what is happening as the light moves through the atmosphere. The value lies in your expanded ability to experience. You have a certain capacity for experience and so does your dog. You might say that humans seem to have a greater capacity for experience than dogs. And to the extent you recognize that capacity as a gift, you might choose to allow it to expand to ever-greater levels.

We often think that when we lose something or someone we love, we are also losing the capacity to love. Not so. The pain of losing is not the *loss* of our love but the *experience* of our love. That gift of experience is not something to bury or squander because it is sometimes painful. In fact, if we allow the pain instead of resisting it, our capacity for experience is expanded. The ability or capacity to love is ours in the same way that the experience of a sunset is ours. That experience can be as individual as fingerprints, but that capacity to experience is what connects us. Our capacity to turn experience that sometimes feels like lead into gold is a gift not an achievement. And it follows a very reliable step-by-step pattern.

All of us have ideas, and any idea is the beginning of a natural cause-and-effect cycle of manifestation. I call it the Natural Experiential Cycle. This absolute cause-and-effect cycle consists of three distinct experiences: idea, action, and learning. An idea leads to action, action creates learning, and learning generates new ideas to begin the cycle again. It is an absolutely reliable cause and effect process, which we often resist even though it is the gift that transforms us.

When you are in resistance, you are probably having a lot of ideas that are not particularly helpful in getting you what you want. You might call them "negative" ideas and they are often your "default" ideas. They probably aren't your best ideas, but when you are challenged, you sometimes "default" to them.

As the result of the Natural Experiential Cycle, those default ideas will follow that step by step pattern and absolutely cause action and learning. That action and learning is not likely to be very productive relative to what you think you want in your life. And as a result of the nature of that natural cause and effect cycle, it is also not logical for you to have a positive inspiring idea in the middle of all that negativity. So what must you do? The answer is to do something illogical. It is the key to grounding the life that inspires you.

The goal of the alchemists was really to perform magic. And all magic has the goal of producing effects or manifesting something through what the dictionary calls incantations. Incantations are the chanting or uttering of words purported to have magical powers like a spell or charm. And that is what this book is all about.

Your incantation is your dream expressed through words. Whether you say you want to open a business, develop a new relationship, or travel to the Far East, you want to perform the magic of change and it all starts with an incantation in the form of your inspired idea put into words.

This book can help you transform you bank account, your relationship status, your spiritual experience, or any other inspired desire that you have. The message you will discover is simply to become more effective with the gifts that you already have so that your transformation can happen naturally. Simple doesn't necessarily mean easy, though, but that's what makes the adventure so exciting.

PART ONE

CLARIFYING WHO YOU ARE

What is my greatest strength? . . .
Imagination.
What is my biggest hurdle? . . .
Self-importance.

Deepak Chopra

Have you ever had an idea that just wouldn't go away? Maybe it related to something you wanted to do in your life, a place you wanted to visit, a business you wanted to build or simply the kind of life you always wanted to live. Have you ever looked back and wondered why many of these ideas never really went anywhere? Part One is about discovering your best ideas, choosing them, and grounding them in action.

Your best ideas are ideas that inspire you. Those ideas are impacted by who you believe you are. If you believe you are a policeman, then you will do policeman-like things. If you believe you are a housewife, then you will do housewife-like things. If you believe you are an honest person, then you will do honest things. The point is that ideas naturally lead to action and so the idea of who you believe you are is very important.

It is important here to distinguish between a *thought* and a *belief*. You might have the *thought* that you want to be a policeman but if at a deeper level you *believe* that you are a dishonest person then that deeper belief will be what determines your actions. If you think you are a policeman but believe you are dishonest, you might do things, which are not typical of the idea of a policeman as someone who is honest and just. Those contradictory beliefs often lie deep in your subconscious and so you might not be consciously aware of why those inspiring thoughts you are having aren't turning into your reality. That contradictory deeper belief can bring about failure in your desire to do the things a successful police officer does.

Getting back to the original question of *why your best ideas never went anywhere* you might now have a sense of why that might be the case. What you thought you wanted to do was overruled by who you believed you were. And that deeper belief is the one that leads to action and results. So, who do you really believe you are?

Rather than get into an internal mental debate with yourself about this question, I suggest a simpler approach. The science of quantum physics suggests that everything including people is just energy. Also, consider that energy is not random, but rather it is by nature creative. You can then believe that you are creative energy. Why creative energy? Because if what you are is creative energy, then what you can do is unlimited.

Certain ideas increase the energy that is you and other ideas decrease that energy. You might find that when you say, for example, "I am an airplane pilot," it tends to increase your energy and when you say, "I am an accounts receivable manager," it tends to decrease your feeling of energy. Or visa versa. Some things excite you and others don't. And accompanying that energy is an organizational or creative aspect.

Getting in touch with that energy is very important, because it can provide a clue to who you can be and what you can do. Your goal then might be to find ideas that feel energetic and in those ideas will come the clarity of who you are at this moment in time. And out of who you are will naturally come what you do which is that creative aspect.

You might note at this point that if you *believe* that you are energy, then that belief will free you to choose to be different things at different times based on what inspires you. You will thus be far less likely to evaluate who you are based on logical beliefs stemming from an old experience.

Part One will help free you to believe that you can be whoever you want to be based on your best, most inspiring ideas.

CHAPTER ONE

START WITH WHAT INSPIRES YOU

The intuitive mind will tell the thinking mind where to look next.

Dr. Jonas Salk

Who are you and why is it useful to have an answer to that question? It is useful to know the answer to that question because who you believe you are determines what you will do. They are not two different things but rather two different aspects of the same thing. An old samurai warrior maxim says, "to know and to act are one and the same." A practical use of that idea is that since we can see in the real world how we are acting, then based on that actual truth, we can infer who, in the invisible world of our mind, we believe we are even though that belief might lie in our subconscious.

If what you are doing in your life is not a reflection of what you want in your life, then you can assume that your deeper belief about who you are is overruling what you think you want. Therefore, in order to change what you are doing in your life, you will want to first change your core belief about who you think you are.

Are you satisfied with *what you are doing* in your career? Are you satisfied with *what you are doing* in your relationships? Are you satisfied with family, community, and your spirituality in terms of *what you are doing?* People who are satisfied and energized with *what they are doing* also believe at a deep level that they are the kind of person *who does that.* Let me expand on an earlier example.

Suppose that you get a job as a police officer. That job has a particular structure and description. That structure has been developed over many years of trial and error by many police departments all across the world. Therefore, what a police officer does has been changed and refined to what we might call a "best practices" model.

By the time you begin your first day on the job, you have probably been trained at a Police Academy and completed basic training. You are able to say "I am a police officer" and you will do those things that you have been trained to do as a result of the belief that you are now a police officer.

Suppose that you complete your first day and go home, change into your civilian clothes, and go to the grocery store to get some food. As you are moving toward the cashier, you notice that someone is pointing a gun at the cashier and demanding money. At that moment in time, you might ask yourself, "Am I a civilian or am I a police officer?" The answer to that question will determine what you do next. Who you think you are at any point in time determines what you do.

If you are a veteran police officer, you probably won't consciously ask the question because the belief that you are a police officer has become so deeply accepted that your response will be automatic. If you are a rookie, there might well be a moment of consideration. The idea that "I am a police officer" might not have moved to a deeper level of belief.

If you say, "I am a plumber," then out of that "being" comes what you do. If you don't know *who you are*, then you probably

14

aren't particularly decisive in *what you do*. Rookie police officers are often not as decisive as veteran police officers because they don't know in an experiential way who they are.

So who are you? Once you accept the idea of yourself as energy, then you can move to ideas of how that energy might be defined in the world. The answer won't come from a logical conclusion, but rather from an energetic discovery. What I mean by that is that as you discover where your energy is, you will at the same time begin to define who you are in those terms.

So for example, if you find yourself excited and energized by dancing you will simply say, "I am a dancer" or "I am a beginning dancer." Or if you are past your dancing prime in terms of age, but dancing still excites you, then you might say, "I am a dance teacher" or "I am a choreographer." If you have it backwards and think that who you are is determined by a current outcome, then you will not make the energetic discovery of doing what inspires you. For example, if you have failed in some way then you might define yourself by your current circumstances and declare yourself to be a failure.

Discover where your energy is and then describe yourself as the person who does the thing that excites you. The belief that "I am a dancer" will result in me doing dancer-like things. Am I really a dancer just because I say I am? I suggest that you forget about whether that statement is conceptually true and instead see the statement as your tool to get you doing the things that excite you. Since at your essence you are just creative energy, then you get to pick how that energy is going to organize itself. You begin that process by choosing whom to believe you are. It is a creative choice not a fact.

It is useful to remember that there are a number of levels to who you are. You might play a number of roles in the world such as the one you play at work, at home, in your personal life, in the community you live in and so forth. At any particular time you might say, "*I am* your father" to a son or daughter. You might also say, "*I am* an electrician" when at work. Who you are in these cases is based on your various roles and your current choice of who you are tells you what to do. Most of who you are sits at a subconscious level and you don't even think about it. But who are you in a deeper sense?

You might say, "I am a man" or "I am a woman." These states of being will tell you what to do in a variety of instances. You might say, "I am an American or a Spaniard." You might say, "I am a Muslim or Christian or Jew." In each case, when you say, "I am," you are starting a Natural Experiential Cycle that moves naturally into action or doing.

People don't do things in a random manner although it might seem that way sometimes. Based on the cause and effect nature of the Natural Experiential Cycle, every action comes from an idea. And that idea always evolves out of the core idea of "who I am." However, the idea of "who I am" does not always reflect the you that is most energetically and therefore, authentically you.

For example, suppose you say, in a moment of frustration, "I am such a loser." Your words might not provide a useful idea of who you are. Whether it is useful or not doesn't matter in terms of its effect in the Natural Experiential Cycle. That idea will still lead to action and learning if you choose to hold on to it as the core idea for a cycle. The way you hold on to it is through belief. You *believe* it's true. You *believe* it is who you are. If you don't believe it is true, then it won't control a cycle. If you say it enough, however, your subconscious will begin to accept it as true and will act on it.

Because of the reliability of cause and effect in the Natural Experiential Cycle, you can find out *who you think you are* by simply looking at the results you have in your life right now. If you want to take two big vacations a year but you have only been getting away for long weekends for the last several years, then you have a situation where what you want is conflicting with who you think you are. Your results are a few short vacations while your desire and your energy is in long, exciting vacations.

At a deeper level, you believe that who you are is a person who only takes short vacations. Why you believe that isn't important. In other words, the fact that you provide good reasons for why you must be a person who only takes short vacations doesn't change the fact that you are creative energy and can organize yourself in a different way. Providing "proof" of why you believe something doesn't make it true: but it does start a creative cycle that is founded on that belief.

That belief about who you are determines what you do. It is absolute because as stated above in the samurai warrior maxim, "to know and to act are one and the same." What you do is a reflection of who you think *and believe* you are.

Where you are in your life is something to embrace and allow. Why would you embrace and allow the idea that you are only having a few short vacations when you want long and exciting ones? Because the reality of your actions is an absolutely trustworthy messenger that will tell you who you think you are. Where you are in your life is a guide to how you are thinking at your deepest levels of belief. Use your current activities as a revealing guide to help adjust your core beliefs so that you choose more effective ones.

For example, if *you are* lonely and alone, embrace and allow that observation. You can even say to yourself "who am I?" And then you can answer, "I *believe* that I am a lonely person." What a gift to be able to simply observe what is happening in your life in order to reveal how you have defined who you are! Is it true that you are lonely person? No. The only thing that is true is that your belief or idea is manifesting. You are an amazing creator. Since you are creative energy, you can hold a different idea of who you are and, manifest or create a different experience if you choose to.

17

I know that a lonely person might be saying to him or herself, "I want to have friends and socialize. People are wrong to think that I want to be lonely. If I could change it, I would." Just remember that you don't get to do what you want in your life by just stating the activity as a desire. To say I want to go to Italy is not enough. I must also believe that I am the kind of person who takes trips like that. You get what you get as the result of who you think (and believe) you are. Choose to be a more inspired you, and you will have a more inspiring experience.

How do you choose to be a more inspired you? From a logical standpoint, you might try to determine who you are by starting from what occurred in the past. Since you are creative energy, however, you are not dependent on the past or what was. Instead, you can reorganize your energy and create something completely new. You can make a quantum leap by looking to a more authentic place for guidance.

Discovering what energizes or excites you connects you to that place. What excites you might or might not excite me. Each of us is unique in terms of what energizes us and so discovering that energy is also connecting to something that is authentic within each of us. Logical truths don't make that same authentic connection. So rather than logically evaluating who you are, you can energetically discover who you are. And the way to do that is to get in touch with how ideas impact you energetically.

Everyone has thousands of thoughts every day. Those thoughts and ideas relate to work, play, relationships, community, spiritual ideas and so forth. With so many thoughts, how can you pick out the best ones? The answer is to recognize ideas that inspire you. How do you recognize those ideas?

First, you look for life. Your best ideas breathe life into you. Next, know that your best ideas are more like discoveries than solutions. Know too, that you are not on this planet to solve problems. You are here for an expanding and amazing experience.

18

Finally, know that your best ideas are rooted in resonance not logic. Logical ideas fit into an already existing experience while resonant ideas make the jump to an unexpected experience. In doing so, they expand your capacity for experience.

A good way to start looking for inspiring ideas is to create a someday/maybe list. A someday/maybe list is a collection of perhaps 100 ideas that represent experiences you might like to have someday. Your someday/maybe list is different from your to do list or next actions list. The difference is that you have not committed to the ideas on your someday/maybe list. You are just brainstorming. Later, you will go over the list from time to time and move some of those ideas onto a current projects list or a next actions list. You might even want to move them onto a 100 things I want to do before I die list. In so doing, you are moving your ideas from possibility to intention.

For now, you will just want to have the ideas on your list meet the criteria of being inspirational. Here are some ways to help you develop that list of ideas

Look for the life in you

The word "inspire" means to "breathe life into." The word "expire" means to "die, exhale, or breathe out." Inspirational ideas breathe life into you. They reflect your energetic essence. How do you know when life is breathing into you? The first thing to check is whether the idea is automatically making something happen just by thinking about it. One of the ways you know that an idea is breathing life into you is that it shows. In other words, your physical body will give clues.

The clues usually show up first as body language. As you talk about an inspiring idea, your eyes might get bigger and brighter. Your face might become more animated with a smile or a look of intensity. You might move forward if you are sitting in a chair or

19

stand straighter and taller if you are standing up. Your heart rate might increase and so forth.

In other words, an inspirational idea will usually cause some kind of action, which is visible to others. You will probably experience it as a feeling of energy and excitement and the initiation of action. Often you won't even consciously know that this physical change is happening.

Inspirational ideas are not static. It takes a lot of resistance to keep an inspirational idea in its conceptual form. If you have ever seen a group of kids come up with an idea to do something fun, you will notice that the idea itself cannot sit still. In other words, the kids will begin to get squirmy and active just thinking about it. They are literally inspired.

As you grew to adulthood, you were probably taught to keep some of those inspirational ideas in their conceptual or intellectual form until you and others evaluated and judged them. Often that evaluation and judgment related to whether your inspired action would somehow make your parents or teachers either uncomfortable or proud.

You are now big boys and girls and your goal is not to preserve someone else's comfort zone. Your goal is to live in your own discovery zone, which is an energetic place that lies outside what we often call the comfort zone. You do that by allowing ideas that inspire you to move into action. Your first action is at the minimum to get those ideas onto your someday/maybe list. Better yet is to get some aspect of them on your next actions list.

Also, as you are building your someday/maybe list, you will want to be aware of something very important. Over the years, some of your best ideas have been imprisoned as concepts; as a result, they might be harder to spot. Therefore, you will have to open your heart a little in order for those ideas to show themselves in a physical way. Look for little clues that those ideas are trying to come to life despite a lifetime of judgment designed to keep them quiet. Those clues might include an increase in interest and energy, a sense of adventure and possible discovery, and a sense of resonance or fit with the idea. Put them on your list.

As you begin to discover the life in you or what brings you to life, you are also beginning to clarify who you are. Don't be surprised if you discover that who you are looks a lot like an idea that you have resisted for many years. The resistance itself suggests some level of energy that is you.

Consider resistance as a kind of reverse energy. The fact that you are resisting suggests that your natural energy wants to do something and your logical self doesn't think you should do it. In order to stop you from doing that something, it will require a kind of artificial energy to combat your natural energy. So, you can sometimes notice what you are resisting and by looking deeper, you can uncover what your natural energy is trying to do.

Look for ideas rooted in resonance not logic

Check your list for resonance by asking yourself how each idea *feels*. Let go of any need to have an idea make sense from a logical standpoint. Go to a more intuitive or gut feel approach and ask yourself if the idea has some kind of energetic feeling around it, good or bad. If you find an idea with a lot of energy that feels in some way negative, there is probably something worth looking into around that idea. Again, that is because there might be some level of resistance. You might say that all energy is positive or creative and there is no such thing as negative energy. So the feeling of negative energy is not really negative energy at all. It is positive energy that is in some way blocked. Here is an example.

Suppose that you have an argument with someone you love and you carry some anger around for the rest of the day. Other people might notice a higher level of emotion in talking with you

21

and they might even say you have some negative energy. In truth, what has happened is that what you thought you wanted seems to be blocked by the person you were arguing with. Your core energy is always positive and the negativity or bad feeling is simply your resistance to what seems to stand in the way. So, by looking deeper at those ideas on your list that seem to have a bad feeling, you might discover the positive aspect or energy fueling that idea. Don't necessarily cross that idea off your list.

Your goal is to discover where your energy is reflected through ideas and those energetic ideas are the ones that are inspirational. Inspirational ideas resonate with the part of you that is creative energy. What does that mean?

Take a moment to look around the space where you are now reading this book. As an exercise, keep you eyes open and don't look at anything red. What most people find is that when I say, "don't look at anything red," they can't help but see everything that is red around them. That is because of resonance. When you hold an idea in mind like "red," your attention automatically tunes in to things that resonate. That can be both things on the physical plane and other ideas on the mental plane. Resonance trumps logic in this case meaning that you will see red even though from a logical standpoint you are telling yourself not to see it. Resonance wins every time. The same applies to an idea like "I am an entrepreneur" or "I am an electrician." Resonance will reveal all kinds of things that resonate with those ideas.

That's why telling a misbehaving child "don't be a bad boy" often doesn't work. Logic says, "don't," but resonance only hears "bad boy." Just as you will focus on red in the exercise above, so everything bad will come to mind for the young boy. Your logic will have the opposite effect from what you wanted.

The ideas on your someday/maybe list will want to come from resonance not logic. Those inspired ideas will show up for you if you plant the source idea of *energy* in your conscious mind.

You won't have to think about whether the ideas make sense. Resonance will do the work for you and discover what logic not only can't see, but also what logic often hides.

Holding on to your best ideas starts with recognizing what constitutes a best idea. Your someday/maybe list should help you start to get a feel for where to look for your best ideas. It won't be a logical process. The source of your best ideas is not logical; it is energetic. To understand that energetic source, it can help if you think in terms of experiential cycles. We all experience ebbs and flows in our energy levels. A greater awareness of our energetic experience puts us in touch with the essence of who we are.

You will always resonate with ideas that inspire or energize you. Why? Because the essence of who you are is energy not logic.

Look for ideas that feel more like discoveries than solutions

As you develop your list, you can check each idea to see if it suggests an experience that is more like a discovery than a solution. Inspiring ideas tend to lead to experiences that feel like an adventure. If you are going to hold on to your best ideas, then make the process an adventure, not a job. To help you consider your list of ideas, and narrow it down to things that are more discovery oriented than solution oriented, you can do several things.

First, ask yourself: are you more interested in an idea because of the opportunity for discovery it offers or because you want to solve a problem? Suppose, for example, that you want to be a doctor. You could look at that idea from two different perspectives. One, you might feel awful about seeing people sick and so you want to solve the problem of illness. The other perspective could be that you find helping people to be an amazing experience. You see it as an opportunity to be close to people and the human experience and that idea energizes you.

23

One looks for value externally and the other looks for value internally. Remember, that your gift is internal like the experience of the sunset.

In the first instance, the idea of being a doctor is based on your view of life as presenting a problem. Your focus is not an expanding internal experience. In fact, because your view is externally focused, it can become limiting. When life seems to be a problem, you feel limited. Your goal becomes getting rid of limitation. To put it differently, what is perceived as external begins to limit what is internal. The problem is that the limitation you are trying to get rid of is self-generated, so the more you focus on it, the more resistant it becomes.

In the second instance, the idea of being a doctor is based on your view of life as an opportunity to discover your own ever-expanding capacity for experience. You view life as the gift of awareness, which is internal, and you intend to share that gift by connecting with others at that core level. It is that sharing of energy that connects us.

I have noticed that many people who find life more of a heavy burden than an amazing experience often take things very literally. By that I mean that there is the assumption that what is spoken or written can represent truth. This literal approach to life reminds me of the saying that "the map is not the territory." Literal people seem like they are endlessly trying to reconcile what is said with their experience. They experience life as a problem and even a paradox. When you place value externally, life can take on the appearance of this kind of contradiction.

Those people have been taught that words accurately represent experience rather than that words are part of expanding experience. Trying to make words accurately represent experience can be an incredibly limiting approach to life. It can make life more of a problem to be solved than a discovery or opportunity to expand the human capacity for experience.

Ultimately, the difference between an idea that is discovery-oriented and an idea that is solution oriented is its source. Where did the idea come from?

The simple answer is that if the idea is discovery-oriented then it is inspired and comes from resonance with your essence or what I call *collective awareness.* Collective awareness goes beyond Jung's collective unconscious, which refers to a knowing that is species-wide in its source. Collective awareness is more of a universal knowing with its source coming from the essential nature of creative energy that we all share.

In her book, *Leadership and the New Science,* Margaret Wheatley says, "Order itself is not rigid or located in any one structure; it is a dynamic organizing energy. When this organizing energy is nourished by information, we are given the gifts of the living universe. The gift is evolution, growth into new forms. Life goes on, richer, more creative than before." [1] It is resonance with this organizing energy that Wheatley refers to - what I call collective awareness - that inspires us and provides that nourishing information in the form of ideas. These are the ideas that lead to discovery of ever-richer experience. These are the ideas we want on our list because they breathe life into us.

Ideas that come from collective awareness are always discovery-oriented rather than problem/solution-oriented. If an idea is solution-oriented, then it probably came from a logical thought process. Its source is a previous conclusion or judgment about something. Those logical conclusions and judgments can be useful in helping manifest an inspired idea, but when looking for inspiring ideas, conclusions and judgments probably aren't so helpful.

Chapter Two will help you better understand the source of your ideas. For now, know that ideas that come from previous logical conclusions usually lead to more of a current experience while ideas that come from collective awareness lead to new and expanding experience.

What if an idea feels exciting but looks like it solves a problem? Every activity could be looked at as solving some kind of problem. A logical case could be made that doctors solve problems. The question of purpose is often confusing until you stop seeing life as an either/or proposition. What does that mean?

Consider the following question. Am I here to solve problems or am I here to have an amazing experience? The question itself presents an either/or proposition. It creates a faulty relationship because it implies that I must choose one or the other. Consider this question instead. Can solving problems be a contributor to an amazing experience? The issue in the second example is one of hierarchy. It does not require that I eliminate one or the other but rather, that one leads and the other follows. Both are allowed.

Consider the organization chart in figure 1. My purpose is to solve problems. Working on problem solving in some instances gives me an amazing or successful experience and working on problem solving in others gives me a bad experience or ends in failure. Sometimes I am successful and sometimes I fail. This is an external orientation when outcomes determine whether I am having an amazing life experience or not.

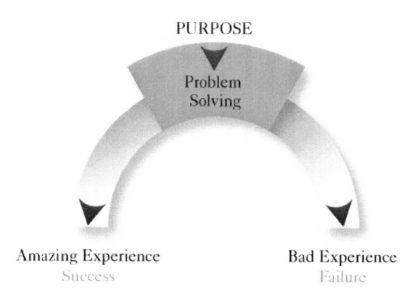

PURPOSE

Problem
Solving

Amazing Experience
Success

Bad Experience
Failure

Figure 1

As suggested by figure 2, my purpose is to have an amazing experience. Part of the make-up of that experience can include problem solving. Thus, problem solving is part of the amazing experience of being alive regardless of whether I judge the effort a success or a failure. In other words, I can fail if my highest purpose is problem solving and I can't fail if my highest purpose is fully experiencing my life and one part of that experience is challenge or problem solving.

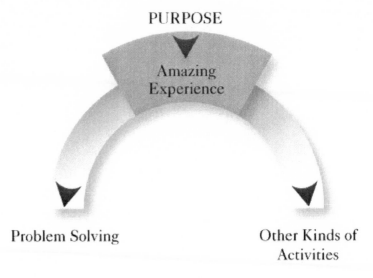

Figure 2

If my primary goal is an amazing life experience (an internal focus), then everything external contributes to it. If my primary goal is to solve problems, then my internal experience is continuously subjected to judgment as to whether it is good or bad based on whether I am successful or not in my external activities many of which I have no control over.

With an internal focus based on an amazing and expanding experience, I will have both joy and pain and together they and all of my other experiences will expand my overall capacity for experience. In each and every activity, however, value lies within me and is never in jeopardy regardless of whether I win or lose. I want to find and hold on to my best ideas because those ideas will put me in the arena of experience associated with what inspires me. In so doing, I will lead an energetic and expansive life. I will stop judging my life and begin living it.

Whether I am building a business, treating a patient or raising a family, my highest goal is not to solve the problems that can be defined in any of those situations. My goal is expansion. Challenging myself to solve problems is part of the nature of that experience, but getting rid of problems is not my primary purpose. To make problem solving my primary purpose is to suggest that value is an external goal to be sought rather than an internal gift to be appreciated.

Thus, the business owner's purpose is not to eliminate competition and sell to everyone. The doctor's purpose is not to eradicate illness, injury or death. And the parent's purpose is not to raise the perfect child that does no wrong. Those kinds of intentions subject your internal experience to external judgments and control.

For each of those people, the highest purpose is to engage in the experience of life. And the way he or she does that is to allow external activities to expand their internal experience. To demand control of external activities is to limit internal experience.

Holding on to your best ideas - the ones that inspire you - is how you focus your experience into an arena that expands and energizes you. Avoiding those inspiring ideas because of fear of failure and pain is an attempt to control your inner experience through outer manipulation. It will keep you from the personal expansion that is your natural gift.

If you have ideas on your list that don't inspire you, then you might wonder if you have some kind of logical reason based on solving the problem of pain or pleasing someone beside yourself. If so, remove the idea from your list. You can always add it back to your list later on if you discover its true source to be inspirational.

As you narrow down your list of inspiring ideas, you might find that some of the ideas that can lead to personal expansion bring up the question of responsibility. You will want to be responsible in what you do and I support that: you will then need to ask, "to whom am I responsible?"

You are probably aware that what you choose to do will always affect others. You do not live in a vacuum no matter how much you might think so. Even if you are homeless, you are part of the mix. Must you then consider your neighbor and your spouse and your kids and the starving children around the world, and the environment, and on and on? How can you possibly make the responsible choice with so many people and things to consider?

Two things might help you with the question of responsibility. First, the source of your best ideas is inspiration not logic. Second, an idea is a general thing offering many ways to take action.

I suggest you be true first to your inspired ideas. Those ideas come from the source of life, which I am calling collective awareness, and it is responsible to choose something that naturally breathes life and energy into you. Out of that creative energy will come your best ideas and those ideas define an arena for you to take action in. You cannot ignore what is naturally energizing to you without taking away your own breath of life. You don't do me any good by reducing the energy you bring to the world. And if I think you must reduce your energy by doing something based purely on logic, then I am probably looking externally for my own energy and value.

Next, I suggest you manage your ideas in a responsible way. What that means is that you challenge yourself. Typically, when I challenge myself I am also challenging others at the same time.

In playing in the arena of my best ideas, I have two rules. One is I don't hurt myself and the other is I don't hurt others. Since I can't predict the outcome of challenging myself, I can only do the best I can in terms of being careful. Hurting myself and hurting others isn't about hurt feelings. Moving out of my

30

comfort zone and into my discovery zone means it might not be comfortable for me or for anyone else involved. Not surprisingly, the place of discomfort is where discovery is most likely to occur. Why? Because it is a place of energy.

If your inspired idea is to be a dancer and you have a husband or wife and three children, it might not be responsible to leave them all and head for New York. It also might be irresponsible to abandon the idea altogether. You manage the idea by getting into the arena and creating a challenge for yourself and possibly for your family. There are many ways you can fulfill your dream of being a dancer without leaving home and heading to New York.

In Jon Krakauer's book *Into Thin Air*, the author tells the story of the Everest expedition that left nine people dead. Krakauer says, "Achieving the summit of a mountain was tangible, immutable, concrete. The incumbent hazards lent the activity a seriousness of purpose that was sorely missed from the rest of my life. I thrilled in the fresh perspective that came from tipping the ordinary plane of existence on end." [2] If you want to be thrilled by a fresh perspective, you will be more likely to have that experience through one of the inspired ideas on your list.

CHAPTER TWO

THINK IN TERMS OF
CYCLES OF EXPERIENCE

I embrace emerging experience. I participate in discovery.
I am a butterfly. I am not a butterfly collector.
I want the experience of the butterfly.

William Stafford

The idea of a cycle is easy enough to think about. As a kid, you might have had the idea to play stickball or some other game. That idea quickly turned to action as you set up bases, got a bat and ball, and so forth. And after playing for a while, the game came to an end. As a result of playing the game, you gained new learning in the form of mastering some new plays or how to hit the ball better. At a deeper level you also gained clarity of who you are not in a fixed way, but in an experiential and energetic way. You might have said, "I am a baseball player and I had the experience of a baseball player." That experience might or might not have been defined as successful, but regardless it was the experience of a baseball player. That clarity can come about as the result of the completion of a cycle.

This cycle is what I call the Natural Experiential Cycle (figure 3). Ideas lead to action. Action leads to learning and learning leads to new ideas that start a new cycle. Within a cycle, each phase leads naturally to the next. Also, one cycle may or may not lead to a repetition of that same cycle again. Kids might play stickball for an hour and then go do something else that is completely unrelated thus starting a new and different cycle of experience.

NATURAL EXPERIENTIAL CYCLE™

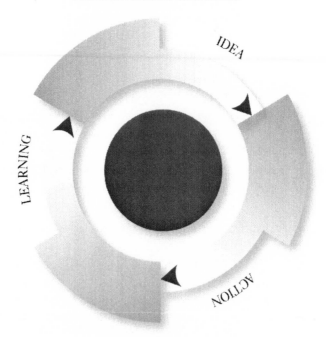

Figure 3

In other words, ideas start Natural Experiential Cycles. Those ideas then turn into action and that action turns into learning. Finally, that learning gives birth to a new idea. For John Krakauer, the idea of climbing Mt. Everest turned into action and a great deal of learning. The experience ultimately led to a thrilling, fresh perspective. That fresh perspective and awareness is the nature of personal expansion. No doubt, part of that experience was very painful because it involved the loss of friends and fellow climbers. Such is sometimes the nature of expanding awareness.

It sounds simple enough and yet people sometimes abandon cycles that are in some way challenging. Those challenges often have many less physically dangerous aspects than climbing Mt. Everest and yet fear can keep them from taking action. Abandoning a cycle that is based on an idea that was inspired or that excited you is abandoning yourself. By this I mean that sometimes when you don't complete full cycles, you can find yourself confused about who you are. This confusion is not related to whether you are a winner or loser. It is related to incomplete experience and the loss of the opportunity for clarity about who you are that comes with completion.

What if the kids on one team in the stickball example became discouraged during the game because they were losing and then they quit? Stopping because of a judgment that they wouldn't be able to win would rob them of the complete experience and the deeper awareness that comes with it. Playing stickball had originally excited them and they gave up on the manifestation of their inspired idea. In doing so, they did not gain the full experience of who they were energetically. As a result, they experienced that part of themselves that held inspired ideas and started action. But they did not gain the clarity of that part of them that completed action and gained new learning and, in doing so, uncovered the awareness of who they are at a deeper level of experience. That deeper level goes beyond a judgment about an experience to the clarity that comes from experience itself.

Thus, action is really your creative idea expanding and manifesting. Learning is the further expansion of that original idea to a level of knowing that connects back with collective awareness or your creative energetic essence. The new idea generated from that creative energetic is a further expansion not of an idea but of experience itself through a new cycle. That new awareness is not more knowledge but simply the capacity for more profound experience that comes from *tipping the ordinary plane of existence on end*. You do that every time you follow an inspired idea, big or small, through the cycle to the revelation of that new awareness. This goes beyond gaining more knowledge. Ultimately, it is about the ability to experience in new and deeper ways.

Going back to an earlier example of experiencing the sunset with the dog, my experience has a richness that, it seems, the dog can never know. This is not an achievement – it is a gift. I only need to complete cycles that are founded on those ideas that inspire me to receive that gift of clarity of who I am. To put it differently, the Natural Experiential Cycle is a cycle of manifestation, not heady logic. It is an ever-expanding cycle not of facts but of energy and experience. Completing the cycle is how you discover a deeper and more fulfilling experience, which brings with it the clarity of who you are.

When you think of an Olympic champion going for the gold, the idea that inspires you might be the image of the runner crossing the finish line with a look of triumph. You feel the champion's fulfillment and sense of being vitally alive. While the athlete may feel a life-long sense of achievement, the real joy is not in the medal. It is in the experience of being able to prepare for and participate in the Olympics and the clarity that such an experience uncovers. That experience provides the athlete a lofty view of existence that can only grow out of inspired ideas. Participating in the Olympics is tipping the ordinary plane of existence on end for the athlete involved.

Not everyone is gifted with the great athletic ability that accompanies qualifying for the Olympics. Everyone is gifted, however, with that same essence of creative energy and the opportunity to gain that clarity of self. So, how can you have such amazing experiences without necessarily winning the Olympic gold medal? The answer is to think in terms of experiential cycles or the Natural Experiential Cycle. How do you do that?

First, understand the difference between a conceptual cycle and an experiential cycle so that you can keep your experience discovery-oriented. Second, know the three phases of an experiential cycle so you can engage fully in your life experience. Finally, so that you can gain the full benefit of your life experience, understand that the value of an experiential cycle goes beyond the individual parts.

Experience vs. concept

We can think about a project or event in any way we want, and we can define the related cycles in any way we want. That definition has a conceptual beginning and end, which does not necessarily coincide with the experiential beginning and end. For example, a foot race may conceptually end at the finish line, but because we lose, we might have an experiential cycle that does not end for days as we painfully replay the outcome.

A conceptual cycle is a logical construction designed to provide definitions, rules, boundaries, and so forth. It is conditional and is actually part of the idea phase of the Natural Experiential Cycle. You might say that conceptual cycles define the temporary rules of a game within which we can experience our self. In fact, a conceptual cycle is a part of a Natural Experiential Cycle. The conceptual cycle could be looked at as the original generation and crystallization of an idea. That concept leads to action.

Full Cycle

The Natural Experiential Cycle involves three general phases that occur in sequence. They are: (1) idea, (2) action, and (3) learning. After new learning, a new cycle starts with a new idea, new action, and again new learning. Personal expansion is *not* the learning that results from that cycle. It is the awareness that occurs as the result of the completed cycle, including the learning, integrated into collective awareness. In other words, learning is part of the cycle but not the goal of your experience.

Let's assume that you decide to apply for a new job. That intention is an expansion of an idea related to who you think you are. For example, you might think that you would like to be a computer programmer. So you go to school to learn the basics and then apply for this new job.

The idea to apply for the job will naturally lead to action and that action will be to fill out an application and send it in for consideration. As a result of sending your application in, a certain result will occur and along with that result will be your new learning. Regardless of whether you get the job or not and regardless of whether the company even responds, you will have new learning. That new learning will naturally be followed by a new idea for you. That is the full cycle opening the door to a new cycle.

A key here is to understand that the new idea does not come directly from the learning in the previous cycle. That learning marks the end of the cycle. The new idea comes from the sum total of all of your experience or collective awareness. Whatever you learned in the application process does not control what you will do next. That is because your next idea is not necessarily the logical extension of what you specifically learned in the process. That new idea is the energetic offspring of collective awareness or everything you have ever experienced. The fact, for example, that someone cuts you off in traffic does not mean you have to respond to that experience directly.

It can be useful to be aware of the full cycle from the standpoint of energetic completion. If you take the action of sending in the application and you never reach some kind of completion, you will probably feel some level of frustration. That frustration is directly related to your energy. Energy wants to complete and renew itself. Lack of completion does not allow that renewal to take place. Without that completion and renewal, the awareness that starts a new cycle is frustrated.

To illustrate, picture yourself watching a movie like *Indiana Jones* or *Star Wars*. Assume that in the middle of the film, the projector begins repeating a scene over and over. Regardless of whether the scene is good or bad, you can guess that it would get boring very quickly. That is because you would be stuck in a cycle that was repeating itself over and over without moving on to a new cycle inspired by a new idea. In other words, each cycle in the repeating segment of the movie is founded on the same idea. Such repetition disconnects you from collective awareness and your creative essence. That disconnect causes you to lose clarity of who you are.

In order to fully appreciate the movie and yourself, you must complete experiences and move on. The value of the experience of the movie does not just lie in the ending or any particular segment. It lies in the whole experience of the movie including all of its parts. With a great movie you might leave the theater saying, "wow, that was amazing."

You might then remember specific scenes that were really fun and others that were scary or sad. Notice that the value of the movie lies in the whole experience. So it is with your life experience. Completing cycles gives your life its rich meaning and expands your ability to experience life at ever-deeper levels.

Getting stuck at any point results in a contraction of experience because the cycle can't reach completion.

Thinking in terms of cycles, you can tackle the things you want to do with the intent of experiencing them in a complete way. Instead of just working to get things done, or being obsessed with the end product that is sometimes called "success," you can come to experience your life in a way where the total experience is greater than the individual parts. What does that mean? It means that you don't pick and choose parts of your experience that seem better than other parts. And you don't allow part of your experience to attempt to control the rest. Instead, you allow the whole of every experience to impact you in the way that expands your capacity to experience your life at ever more fulfilling levels. In other words, your goal is to treat all of your experiences as expansive rather than defining or limiting. One way to look at it is that losing a business, for example, can feel very limiting while at the same time be very expansive from an experiential perspective. Your goal is to become an expert at supporting your own Natural Experiential Cycles, which is how you support your own personal expansion.

Understanding and living those cycles more fully can make your everyday experiences as amazing as winning a gold medal. Remember that the capacity for amazing experience lies within you and not in the external world. It is more a choice of *how you will use your capacity to experience* the world around you in this moment, than *your ability to obtain something in the future that you think will be amazing*. You hold the key and that key can not only provide amazing experiences, but also easily put you in the winner's circle. Most importantly, it will give you the clarity of who you are not as an idea but as the experience of creative energy.

Sometimes you might resist completing those Natural Experiential Cycles and in so doing not allow yourself to have an expanding life experience. It's like replaying the best or worst scene in a movie over and over. Go for all the pieces in order to expand your experiential capacity because the real purpose of the cycle is not to succeed or fail. It is to have an experience where you feel connected to your own creative energetic and the inspiration it provides. Stay consciously aware of the full cycle of a Natural Experiential Cycle and you will be better able to manage your energy.

Learning vs. Awareness

Awareness is an open cycle connected to creative energy while learning is a closed cycle connected to itself (a repeating cycle). Awareness provides the opportunity for a quantum leap to something previously undefined and not experienced while learning repeats or extends what is already known.

When, for example, I learn that two plus two equals four, I have created a conditional circle of logic that can be used over and over in order to reach a certain conclusion or outcome. It is guaranteed because I have stated the conditions that will create that result. So when I learn how to build a bridge, I have come to understand how to create a specific outcome. That learning can be very useful.

Awareness as I define it is quite different. It is not designed to create a definite conceptual outcome. Rather, it is designed to jump outside the outcomes that I currently understand by connecting to creative energy. That jump and discovery directly affects my capacity to experience. The effect is an expansion of that capacity. Growing awareness leads to experience at a deeper, more profound level.

Consider an example of how learning and awareness occur in your life. Suppose that you have an idea for a business or any goal you might have. The Natural Experiential Cycle suggests that your idea will naturally lead to action and that action will lead to learning. Then a new idea will be generated starting a new cycle.

You can think about a project or event in any way you want, and you can define the related cycles in any way you want. That definition has a conceptual beginning and end, which does not necessarily coincide with the experiential cycle.

Because of your idea and its accompanying cycle of experience, you arrive at new learning. The new learning relates to your concept for the cycle and how closely you matched it in the real world. The new awareness relates to your overall experience and connects to your energetic essence and its nature. You might have learned how to improve your business relative to your conception of it. The overall experience, however, might have led to an awareness of your energy and its creative possibilities. Learning is always relative to a closed concept so it is limiting, although often useful. Awareness is always connected to collective awareness or creative energy and so it is expanding and unlimited. Learning asks, "what did I do right or wrong within this cycle?" Awareness asks, "what inspires me now, and how can I begin a new cycle?"

Because ideas lead to action and results, you may as well make that original idea a good one. In fact, it makes sense to choose an idea that is your best one. By finding your best idea, regardless of what has come before, you naturally tap into what makes you most inspired and alive. You connect to that part of yourself that is unlimited. Motivation flows into all your activities, and your outlook becomes positive and attractive to new friends, opportunities, and experiences. By living in the field of your best ideas and greatest inspiration, you make your own good fortune whether pursuing an adventure, invention, or a business. Breathing in your natural vitality, you gather piece by piece the insights, connections, and serendipitous discoveries that lead to unprecedented breakthroughs in achievement.

This is not to say your path will be strewn with rose petals everywhere you step. Whether your experience is hard or easy from day to day will matter little when you know the fulfillment of expressing your vital life force by living your best ideas. At the same time, when you exude enthusiasm and well being, when you live with purpose guided by awareness (rather than learning), you attract to yourself resonant circumstances, friends, and opportunities. You shine with awareness, and your world forms itself around your best idea. You gain a level of useful influence through learning and you maintain the clarity of who you are through awareness.

Having chosen your best idea as a starting point, you might jot down something such as: *write a book about grounding the life that inspires you.* With that idea, your Natural Experiential Cycle takes over. In other words, you naturally move into action. In this example, you might write down some ideas for the book or call some associates for suggestions on how to proceed and where to get some direction in writing the book.

Here is a key point: The transition from idea to action is not a decision that you make although you might often think of it that way. Ideas naturally lead to action and manifestation. If the idea is the in-breath, then action is the out-breath, the natural consequence. If you have any decision to make, it is whether you will choose to hold your breath or let it out into the world. Holding the breath is a metaphor for the resistance that can show up in the transition from idea to action, and learning to work with this resistance effectively is an important part of achieving a fulfilling, meaningful experience.

Ideas are always becoming and do not exist in a vacuum. It might feel like you could have an idea in a purely conceptual manner, but in reality, ideas are experiential: they cannot stand still. Ideas are vitally alive, and they want to become something and manifest in the observable world. You experience that manifestation as action.

In other words, an integral aspect of every thought or idea is energy. Energy is dynamic or active so every idea also has momentum or movement at some level. Ideas are not inactive, although you might have come to believe that they can be. Some ideas have very powerful and obvious energy and some have very subtle energy.

For example, perhaps you get the idea to take a three-month trip around the world. You feel the energy of the idea wanting to move in and through you into what you might call the real world. If the idea excites you and yet you don't do anything about it, you may feel it tug toward action. If you fear leaving your job for three months, you may experience a conflict between your holding back and the idea's natural desire to manifest and expand through action. This conflict between holding back and moving forward is resistance, and it is a natural part of the cycle. In fact, without resistance, you would have no experience at all. So to enjoy a meaningful experience, you must learn to work with resistance effectively.

The most important thing to grasp at this point is simply this: ideas and action are *one and the same*. When you have an idea, you also have action in its initial manifestation and it will continue to grow unless you resist it.

After you have allowed an idea to grow in action and manifestation, you discover through the Natural Experiential Cycle that action naturally leads to learning. Action does not want to continue forever. It wants learning and expanded awareness. The point where learning turns into awareness is experiential completion. For example, your desire to climb a mountain comes to a natural end. After completion, you might naturally want to return home, put your feet up by the fire, and celebrate the

44

adventure. There, you review your learning and then allow the integration of your experiences into new awareness.

A new cycle will start as the natural result of the integration of your experience into collective awareness. For example, after completing the Mt. Everest climb, Krakauer experienced a new level of awareness that he described as a "fresh perspective that came from tipping the ordinary plane of existence on end." That new awareness may lead to climbing a different mountain, doing something very mundane, or writing a book, as Krakauer did. A new idea is born that naturally moves toward action once again. Without the completed experience, that new idea cannot be born and you will never experience that new you. Regardless of what comes next, you will be changed. Inspired experience changes you in a process of personal expansion without which you will not have the thrill of fresh perspectives.

CHAPTER THREE

USE CAUSE & EFFECT FOR RESULTS

You are searching for the magic key that will unlock the door to the source of power; and yet you have the key in your own hands, and you may use it the moment you learn to control your thoughts.

Napoleon Hill

The Natural Experiential Cycle is very reliable. It is guaranteed to naturally produce personal expansion and ever more profound experience. But those cycles are a little like fire; you can get burned. That expansion can include getting burned, but it isn't necessary to keep experiencing that pain if you allow what is natural to work the way it is meant to work. Typically, once you are burned you understand how fire works and you are careful not to get burned again. With the Natural Experiential Cycle, however, it seems that some people never learn how it works. And so they continue to get burned over and over again.

Here is how the cycle works. Ideas cause action, which causes learning. Once integrated, that cycle impacts collective awareness and the result is a new idea. Here is the profound learning that can keep you from getting burned over and over again. Be careful what you choose to believe. What you believe will turn into ideas that will start that very reliable cycle. If your beliefs are founded on fear, then you will experience what you fear over and over again in one form or another.

The cycle guarantees it. If, however, your beliefs are founded on creative energy coming from collective awareness or inspiration, then you will experience personal expansion and the thrilling perspectives that come with it. That includes getting burned every once in a while, but more importantly, it will produce a life experience that reflects your creative energetic essence. That life is the one you want.

Concept of Cause and Effect

When you think of cause and effect, you might think of something like billiard balls bouncing off each other. One ball rolls across the table and hits another. It appears as if the action of the original ball is causing the specific action of the other ball.

If you believe that cause and effect works that way, you then might draw the conclusion that your actions can actually cause specific actions in the external world and that you can, therefore, control outcomes and get what you want. This, however, might not be the most useful way to think about cause and effect.

You might have experienced a time when you created great plans and began to take action only to have all kinds of unexpected and undesirable results despite your best efforts. If you felt frustrated, it is probably because you had the idea that there was a law of cause and effect whereby you could control external effects (i.e. your actions could cause specific results in the world). Here is a different way to think of cause and effect, which can't fail.

Think of cause and effect as a process of manifestation that is by nature, personally expanding. In other words, think of cause and effect as a process in which ideas or thoughts that start in your mind cause your actions in the physical world. As a direct result of that process of manifestation, new learning emerges for you and for others. The new learning is not limited by your original idea and vision for how you think it will manifest. Others influence and are influenced by you as the idea manifests in the

48

external world. Your learning includes external responses by people and things to your actions. You influence things in the external world, but you cannot control them. As a result, you cannot predict your learning. If you could, it would not be called learning.

Consider the example of billiard balls bouncing off each other. Quantum physics has demonstrated that cause and effect in the external world can only be thought of in terms of probability. Why? Because the external world at its essence is also creative energy and it goes through the same Natural Experiential Cycles that you do. As a result, another person doesn't do things based on what you do; rather, he or she does things based on his or her own awareness, which includes but is not limited to you and the things you do. Their new idea comes from collective awareness not just your actions and their learning. The essence of that awareness is creative not responsive. Collective awareness is creative energy. As a result, external results are best thought of in terms of probability rather than direct cause and effect.

So, for example, again picture a group of young people saying something like "hey, let's play stickball!" What happens next? The youngster immediately picks up a stick and tells someone else to pitch the ball. You can see that what was an idea, "let's play stickball," quickly transitions into action in the observable world. It is a natural process of ideas causing actions. And as a direct result of the actions, the kids then gain new learning in playing the game regardless of who wins and who loses. That experience in turn adds to collective awareness.

What if the kids plan on playing six innings but quit after playing only three innings? There might have been the probability that the kids would play six innings when the game started but as the result of action and learning, that outcome changed. The expected cause and effect in the external world did not occur. Does that mean that the absolute nature of experiential cause and effect did not occur? The answer is no. Experiential cause and effect is absolute. The kids had an idea, which turned into action and created new learning.

Remember that the idea of the game as lasting six innings does not necessarily match the experiential cycle. If the kids had the idea of playing, took action to play, learned something and then completed the game experientially, it was because they were ready to move on to something new: the cycle was complete for them. If one of the boys was disappointed that everyone else quit, then he might hold on to that experience for hours or days until he was able to experientially let go and move on in his own present awareness. Regardless of how long it takes, the Natural Experiential Cycle of cause and effect rules. But what about billiard balls and other inanimate objects?

We know through quantum physics that the two billiard balls never actually touch each other. Rather, each is an energy field and those energy fields influence each other as they move closer together. You can think of the interaction of those energy fields as the "awareness" of the balls even though it is quite different from the awareness we associate with living things. The new action that then occurs results from a change in the energy patterns or redefined energy of each ball. If you stretch your mind, that redefined energy can be thought of as a new idea that in turn determines the new action of each ball. That new "idea" is the result of redefined energy not one action specifically causing another. You can consider that since both balls are essentially energy, each one has its own ability to change or move built in. One ball does not move the other. It simply influences the ways in which the movement of the other balls is effected.

Another way to look at the same scenario is that the ball that appears to be at rest is actually moving. It is only at rest relative to the pool table. If you were standing on the moon and looked at the billiard ball, it would look like both the ball and the billiard

50

table were both moving relative to your fixed position on the moon. Also, there is internal movement where the atoms that make up the ball are constantly in motion. Each billiard ball has its own energy and is continuously in motion.

The energy of the second ball includes both internal movement and movement relative to the first ball. As those two energy fields get closer together, each influences the other. The natural cause and effect cycle does not predict the outcome of energy fields influencing each other; rather, it predicts the process of manifestation that will naturally occur as energy interacts and awareness expands. Ideas or defined energy, will lead to action in the physical world, which will lead to learning and then expanded awareness, which will begin the cycle again with a new idea or defined energy. This cycle is the cycle of collective awareness expanding through the Natural Experiential Cycle.

In order to effectively use the concept of the Natural Cause and Effect Cycle, it is important to understand where your control lies and where it does not. The example of the billiard balls is meant to have you consider the idea that since everything is energy and all energy is creative by nature, then external control is not an option. Even with inanimate billiard balls, anomalies or unexpected results do occur. In a way, every aspect of the universe, including billiard balls, has a mind of its own because it has built-in creative energy.

Another way to look at the issue of cause and effect in the external world is to consider our attempt to perceive that external world and how accurate our perceptions are. In the book, *Margins of Reality,* authors Robert Jahn and Brenda Dunne say, "All of these [quantum theories] concede a degree of paradox in human perception of physical processes and suggest that physical theory is less a statement of abstract reality than of our ability to acquire information about that reality." [3] If that is true, then the Natural Experiential Cycle and the cause and effect nature suggested in

51

that cycle can be more useful than a theory of external cause and effect. That is because rather than creating conceptual conclusions about our experience and possibly getting stuck on those conclusions, it addresses a process of simply allowing that experience to expand naturally so that it isn't ruled by those conclusions.

The conclusion that you can control experience can lead to resistance. Resistance is resistance to the natural cycle, not to the things that seem to get in the way. And it is based on the fear that your experience will be painful in some way. Resistance starts as a battle of ideas. If you have experienced mind chatter, then you know what resistance feels like. It is a battle of ideas in your mind based on logic that seeks a way to avoid pain by controlling external things and people.

What we typically think is that an action is caused by a decision to act on an idea. In other words, ideas and actions are two different things connected by a decision. In fact, the youngster picking up the stick to play stickball doesn't make a decision to take action. Taking action is an automatic and natural aspect of having an idea. Our option or choice only relates to the choice of an idea. If we fear what might happen in the external world, then that logical battle of ideas occurs. That can happen at any point in the Natural Experiential Cycle and can interrupt the flow of expanding awareness as a result.

In some cases, the new idea is actually born out of the new awareness gained in a completed cycle even though the completed cycle doesn't match the conceptual cycle. The boys who ended their stickball game in the third inning instead of the sixth inning might have done so because the experience was complete for them and they had a new idea (like going to get something eat) that inspired them. But how do you know if an idea comes from the authentic source of collective awareness or it grows out of fear and resistance to pain? The answer lies in the *feeling* of resistance.

The feeling of resistance occurs as the result of an external control issue. It is fear-based and since it is a feeling, it contains some added energy. That increase in energy directed at not doing something as opposed to energy that is inspired to do something is a key. If the kids say, "hey, let's play stickball" and everyone is excited to do that, then there is energy in what they want to do. They don't draw up a long list of what they emphatically don't want to do.

If those same kids say, "Whatever we do, let's definitely not play tag!" then their motivation is resistance that has resulted from fear of something. There is a good chance that they had some kind of Natural Experiential Cycle around playing tag that is not complete. When events are experientially complete there is no energy left because experiential completion is energetic completion. It is almost as if those other options don't exist at all because they contain no energy.

When a Cycle is interrupted by resistance or founded on an idea that is fear-based, it can be useful to look for the source of that idea because that source is probably a logical conclusion of some kind. It typically indicates an incomplete experiential cycle and it will tend to continue to create cycles based on logical ideas designed to control something external. That desire for control usually comes from memories of old painful experiences that have not been let go to integrate into collective awareness. It will typically interfere with a current authentic and inspiring idea and cycle.

It is very natural to apply logic to how you go about doing things and to use what you have learned in order to do things in new ways. Using logic in that way isn't a sign of resistance to errors or traumas that occurred in the past. It is the nature of expanding awareness. The sign that you look for in a cycle isn't choosing to do things more effectively; it is a spike in energy around something that logically challenges the whole idea. That

53

can be a sign of resistance, fear, and an old incomplete cycle. That old incomplete cycle can sabotage personal expansion in your current life.

When you see cause and effect as an external possibility for control, you live in resistance and fear. Your goal is to control experience so you can avoid pain that is incomplete and you find yourself in a constant battle of ideas. You are often past or future-oriented, either rehashing old experiences or trying to predict and control your future.

When you see cause and effect as the natural process of expanding awareness, your goal is experiencing your own creative energy. You typically are focused on one idea at a time that inspires you and you are very present-oriented. And you are able to let go of each experience, good or bad, in order to make way for something new.

Returning to the example of the billiard balls, it could be said that they (the billiard balls) have little in the way of expanding awareness. Even though balls hit each other, they never really seem to demonstrate any learning and never do something different like getting out of the way as a cue ball approaches. Maybe it's because they just can't let go of an idea of who they are, i.e. old energy patterns. That is a topic for a different book, but a point can be taken nonetheless. You will become something new as the result of a new inspired idea if you allow yourself to move through Natural Experiential Cycles. That cause and effect cycle is natural and requires no control on your part. Mostly it requires letting go of control and simply connecting with your own creative energy.

Alfred Russel Wallace said, "The marvelous complexity of forces which appear to control matter, if not actually to constitute it, are and must be mind-products." [4] So, billiard balls are mind-products just as you are. If you become too resistant and fearful, you can become unchanging in ways similar to billiard balls. In

54

that case, you can feel like you are at the mercy of external events (other billiard balls) bouncing you all over the place. Your relationships might remain unfulfilling, your career stagnant, and your personal sense of expansion missing. Someone might say to you, *"why don't you get out of the way and allow the relationship, career, or yourself to change?"*

In order to make your experiences fulfilling and expansive, it can be helpful to understand the concept of the natural cause and effect process and use it every day to reveal your best, most life giving ideas. That revelation of inspiring ideas occurs in a Natural Experiential Cycle. Hold on to your best ideas and look underneath any ideas that try to do battle with them for signs of destructive fear rather than creative support.

A key aspect of the concept of natural cause and effect is to remember how I defined the difference between learning and awareness. In the Natural Experiential Cycle, both learning and awareness occur although awareness does not occur at the same level as learning. It is important to know the difference because your best or inspired ideas come from awareness rather than something specific you have learned. Consider the following martial arts example to illustrate.

Suppose that you choose to study a martial art like Aikido and in your first class you learn how to block a punch aimed at your upper body. In the next class, you learn how to block a punch to your head and in the third class you learn how to block a punch aimed at your lower body. Each is a specific technique that you learned for a specific purpose. Each is taught in a specific way and practiced over and over in exactly the same way.

Learning is the creation of fixed ideas and accompanying actions that are designed to produce certain outcomes. Learning is conditionally useful meaning that it is only useful if everything external occurs in a controlled way. So, learning how to block a punch to your head is only useful under those conditions where someone is aiming a punch at your head exactly in the way you were taught. Learning is conditional and inflexible.

Awareness takes learning and combines it with other experience in a kind of magical way. It takes learning that is conditional and makes it unconditional. Awareness takes all three lessons of how to block punches and integrates them in a way that makes any one or combination of them available at any time based on the situation. Not only does it make each available it also allows variation of them in ways that were not taught and it allows you to not block at all if you choose. Awareness is an order of change above the absolute cause and effect of a Natural Experiential Cycle meaning; it is not controlled by any one cycle. You can do whatever inspires you regardless of the conclusions that occurred in any previous cycle.

That is why I say that in the final phase of the Natural Experiential Cycle, you will let go of learning and allow it to integrate into collective awareness. That collective awareness is the collection of not just everything you have learned but everything you have experienced including experiences that you are not even conscious of. Awareness removes the boundaries and definitions that you have created as learning and makes experience available in a way that allows creation of something completely new, defined only by your current creative energy.

Luther Burbank said, "When simple cells become joined together, . . . they exhibit organizing forces in new directions which were impossible by any of the individual cells." [5] So it is with learning when it is allowed to blend in its entirety into collective awareness. I don't need to draw a conclusion in order to have an expanded capacity for experience. In fact, I must let go of conclusions in order for personal expansion to occur.

This is exactly the fork in the road that determines whether your cycles will be fulfilling. Think of the cells that Burbank refers to above as being like completed cycles. When you reach

56

experiential completion, then that experience, when integrated into your collective awareness, will "exhibit organizing forces in new directions which were impossible by any of the individual" experiences or any of the individual things that you learned.

In other words, when a completed cycle of experience, including the learning, moves into your collective awareness, you are transformed. The way you are transformed is through the new idea that is generated which would have been impossible by any of the individual conceptual conclusions.

Past traumatic experiences are actually a form of learning that can get you stuck. You try to "learn" how to make sure it will never happen again. It is like getting punched in the upper body and then spending all of your time practicing your upper body block to ensure it won't happen again. The problem is that since the upper body block is only useful in certain conditions, you might find yourself recreating those conditions over and over in order to be sure you are safe.

Once old learning that is stuck in an old cycle is allowed to reach experiential completion, then that new level of awareness can free you to ideas that come from your source of collective awareness. That source will always provide your best ideas and it is also more likely to keep you safe.

You might suspect that you are depending on learning instead of awareness if you are engaged in repetitive behavior that is unfulfilling. Often, it is hard to see how you have attached to some kind of learning that won't allow completion of a Natural Experiential Cycle and the release of the energy it still holds. Sometimes, it can be very useful to get highly qualified outside help to reveal that cycle that you are stuck in and help bring it to experiential completion.

Only then can new inspirational and transformational ideas make themselves known in an unresisting mental environment. As a result, discovering your best ideas will require ongoing attention to bringing action to completion not from a conceptual standpoint but from the standpoint of experience.

Remember that completion of a cycle really is not just about completion of the concept or the way you have conceptually defined a particular cycle. It has to do with completion of the *experience*. This is a Natural Experiential Cycle.

For example, as I said earlier, if I define a cycle as running a foot race and I define the finish line as the point of completion of the cycle, then I have defined a conceptual point of completion. If, however, I lose the race and I am bummed out for days after the race, then from an experiential standpoint, the cycle is continuing for me although I crossed the finish line days before. In the same way, if I fall and don't complete the race, I can still complete the race experientially and allow the experience to be complete and integrated in collective awareness.

The Natural Experiential Cycle is a reliable cause and effect process. Ideas turn into action and action turns into learning. And once energetically complete, the cycle as a whole can move into collective awareness to support personal expansion. An experiential cycle cannot be complete without completing this sequence of manifestation. You do not have to complete a conceptual or logically created cycle in order to have experiential completion. Also, it is possible to have conceptual completion without having experiential completion. You will not have ongoing personal expansion if you do not complete things experientially because your best ideas will continue to do battle with old, experientially incomplete ideas.

The effort to control external events in order to avoid pain is the sign of old incomplete experiential cycles. Although you do influence things in the external world, there is no absolute cause and effect relationship between you and other people and things. There is only probability. The things that you do every day influence the world around you, but they do not control it.

Growing or expanding awareness through Natural Experiential Cycles is an absolute while conceptual cycles are just useful illusions creating arenas within which that personal expansion can occur.

Experience of Cause and Effect

The experience of cause and effect can be quite frustrating at times. It can, in fact, feel like your life is being controlled by some external force or fate that keeps you in financial straits or relationship disasters or something similar where you aren't getting what you think you want. What can you do to begin to create what you want in life?

Knowing about the cause and effect process of a Natural Experiential Cycle, you might decide to start each day with an affirmation that is designed to plant an idea in your mind that will result in a rewarding cycle. You might, for example, say each morning, "I am a financial wizard making more and more money each day." You would then further expect that your affirmation would transition into action and new learning. That cycle should result in an ever growing awareness of money and how to make more and more of it. But you find yourself year after year struggling to make ends meet. What is the problem?

The answer is that the cycle is experiential not conceptual. It is based on your experience of life, not your concept of it. You can create all the conceptual affirmations you want, but if you have an old cycle that is not experientially complete, then you will continue to repeat any judgments or conclusions about that cycle as the idea for your new cycles. In other words, you will create new ideas that will help you continue to experience that old feeling of failure. As a result, you will remain in that old experiential cycle.

What that means is that if you've ever had an experience where you judged yourself unable to make money as the result of some kind of inadequacy, or you judged money as a bad thing, then that judgment, if believed, will continue to be the new idea for current cycles relative to money making. Unless you are able to let go of that negative conclusion and belief, then the experience cannot integrate into your collective awareness in a way that is useful. As a result, you will continue to experience various versions of that experience instead of what you want now.

The Natural Experiential Cycle is a creative cycle and you are a creative being. The fact that you are manifesting a reality of unrewarding relationships, for example, does not indicate that you are not creative: it indicates that you are.

Why would individuals purposely create unrewarding relationships or financial struggle? They do so because they have described an old relationship or financial experience in a way that has become the founding idea for current relationships and money management. And they have attached the description of those things so closely to the old incomplete experiences that they have come to believe the description is true.

Actually, their description of the old relationship has no more validity than the current description of what they would like to have as true. Descriptions and definitions (including those in the subconscious) are not true: they are creative. They are creative because they begin a creative cycle. They are the first phase of the Natural Experiential Cycle and they create action. So, you might want to consider how you define and describe your experiences. Or, as a more useful approach, you might want to consider whether your definitions and judgments are true or just creative.

Language can be a very tricky thing because it can have the appearance of truth. The truth of language, however, is always conditional. In the same way that resonance (which is unconditional) will always trump logic (which is conditional), so

60

too, will an idea that you believe is true, be the basis for a cycle regardless of what you conceptually want to be true. Incomplete experiential cycles, resulting from judgment and conclusions, will continually reproduce the experience until they are allowed to integrate into collective awareness.

The way you have defined an old, abusive relationship is not true; but it can be creative. That creative definition might have been useful and appropriate at the time it was created. It might not be so useful now. That is why you will want to let go at the end of a cycle so that the experience can be complete. A complete experience has no judgments around it that are believed to be true and it has no energy. It just is.

Letting go of any judgments allows you to start a new cycle with fresh ideas and language to express them that is creative rather than true. That fresh language will begin to create what you want. It cannot fail to do so unless you have a sub-conscious belief about an old experience that is actually the founding idea for your current experience. Because of the cause and effect nature of an Experiential Cycle, that old belief or judgment that still carries energy will ensure that you will continue your old experience in all kinds of new ways.

You can think of a judgment as the attachment of language and ideas to an experience in a way that incorrectly connects the truth of the experience to the words that seem to describe it. If I asked you to define love, could you ever find the words that accurately expressed the experience of love? The answer is no.

When my wife died of cancer and my daughters and I stood in a reception line after her service, a man came up to me to pay his respects. He had tears in his eyes and opened his mouth to say something and then just stopped. He finally said, "I don't know what to say" and walked away.

Unknowingly, he had said exactly the right thing. Of all the caring things said to me that day, his comment was the only one that has stayed with me. The depth of his feeling was as clear as the tears in his eyes. His awareness that no logical order could be brought to this event released me from my own effort to answer the question - why did this happen?

Letting go of traumatic experiences like that is often a long process. It was for me. As I look back, however, I can clearly see that the real progress happened through resonance rather than some strategy and plan. In other words, that man intuitively knew that a judgment or conclusion about the experience of losing my wife would never accurately encompass what had happened. In fact, such conclusions rather than completing the experience can sometimes prolong it if they are held on to as a truth. Traumatic experiences cannot be defined in an accurate or truthful way. They can only be allowed to move into collective awareness where they can add to life through the expansion of your capacity for experience. Letting go opens a space for resonance to occur that can bring you fully present.

Conclusions and judgments can actually keep challenging experiences present for years by creating ideas and language that will become the foundation for future creative cycles. To allow yourself to be creative in new and fresh ways is to allow yourself to have new and expanding experiences. The way you do that is to let go of any conclusions or judgments (learning) about your past experience. Instead, let new ideas surface from that resonant place of collective awareness. It is that place that is unconditional and limitless and it only exists in this present moment.

Embrace the idea that there are no words that can accurately describe your experience. Words are not true: they are creative. To have the expanding experience that you want, start with words and language that come from collective awareness. Then you will experience the power of the natural cause and effect cycle. If you start a cycle with ideas that come from old judgments, then your experience will be very similar to that old cycle. When that happens, you can get burned over and over again.

The experience of personal expansion that comes with Natural Experiential Cycles is one of discovery and energy. The experience of personal contraction that comes with repetition of old cycles is one of stagnation and diminishing energy. Believe that *what you think matters* because it is those ideas and language that will start your next Experiential Cycle. Resonant ideas coming from collective awareness will be empowering and ideas that come from old judgments and conclusions will be disempowering.

Using Cause and Effect Cycles

Cause and effect cycles are very reliable because they are natural. You don't control them. As a result, your role in life is not to create something. Rather, it is to choose a path where your natural creativity is placed in an arena that inspires you and then work with your resistance to the natural process that then occurs. That natural process will, if you let it, expand your experience. It will do that through a process that we might call *discovery*.

When, for example, you find someone you like and begin to spend time with him or her, a natural creative process is occurring. That creative process is a moment-to-moment occurrence. The way that you use a cause and effect cycle is to stay present in each moment. Without present consciousness, the cycle can default to an old cycle for the ideas that create action. The result will be the recreation of an old experience.

The process of staying conscious is not about using logic to ensure that what happened before won't happen again. Doing that will almost ensure that it will. Staying conscious is more about feeling than thinking. Hold on to your inspired idea of who you are in a relationship and then just allow intuition to guide you. Does caring and supporting someone in relationship inspire you?

If that is where your energy is, then hold on to those notions and allow action to naturally follow. That action will be connected to the energy that is you and that awareness is the consciousness you want.

If you are someone who has ever wondered why your relationships all seem to have similar unfulfilling experiences, you might ask yourself whether you are staying conscious in the relationship. The same applies to your professional life, your health and fitness, and so forth. You use cause and effect cycles effectively by staying conscious or present in the cycle. By doing that, you use cause and effect cycles in a way that creates personal expansion, win or lose.

Consider the nature of your body. Suppose that you decide you want to have your body look more muscular. How can you use cause and effect cycles to make that happen? Since cause and effect cycles are natural, you can assume that an effort to lift weights will not accomplish the transformation alone. Instead, you know that creating that body will occur naturally. You also know that your job is essentially to choose the path of who you are, and then stay conscious throughout the cycle by being connected to your energetic, inspiring idea. The rest is a cause and effect process that will take care of itself naturally. The idea will turn into action: for example, you might start lifting weights. Action will turn into learning and then growing awareness. So you might find yourself adding weight to your barbells or increasing the number of repetitions as time goes by or you might find yourself changing to rock climbing or world travel instead. This process of personal expansion is natural and as long as you stay conscious in the experience, you will manifest change according to your creative energy awareness or what you truly want.

Deepak Chopra gives an explanation that can be helpful here.

At any point in the bodymind, two things come together — a bit of information and a bit of matter. Of the two, the information has a longer life span than the solid matter it is matched with. . . This fact makes us realize that memory must be more permanent than matter. What is a cell, then? It is a memory that has built some matter around itself, forming a specific pattern. Your body is just the place your memory calls home. [6]

The bit of information that Chopra refers to is, in the Natural Experiential Cycle, the idea that starts a cycle of creation. It is that idea that determines the cause and effect cycle that manifests, for example, a more muscular body. It can do that if the idea occurs at the level of belief. That belief is not one founded on "fact" but rather, one founded on the nature of creative energy as your essence. If you don't hold that conscious "belief" throughout the cycle, you can default to old subconscious beliefs and information. That old information will then continue to manifest and you will naturally recreate the body you thought you wanted to change.

In her book, *Leadership and the New Science*, Margaret Wheatly says, "All life uses information to organize itself into form. A living being is not a stable structure, but a continuous process of organizing information." [7] Since ideas are the organizing process of life, you can see that using the natural cause and effect cycle can do two things. First, if you hold on to an idea, energy (your essence) will organize around that idea naturally creating form. If you are starting a business, then you can see that determining and holding on to a central idea for that business will naturally result in energy forming around the idea. That energy will look like products, services, vendors, customers, advisors, and so forth.

You might also see that if you change that central idea for the business repeatedly, you will disrupt the energy that was beginning to form around the original idea. So the way you use natural cycles is to hold on to those ideas that create what you like and let go of those ideas that create what you don't like.

If you want to build a business and you keep changing the central or governing idea of that business, don't expect the business to grow. By changing that idea, you are continually disrupting the energy that is forming around it and starting over. The same is true for your physical body. Your physical stature is influenced by the information or ideas that are persisting in your mind. Hold on to those ideas and your body will naturally recreate based on that information. Let go of those ideas and allow a new and inspired idea to become the organizing force and action will naturally follow that will create something new.

In the process of creating something new, there can be a conflict between old ideas and the new idea. That conflict will cause resistance. If you don't stay conscious and present in the natural cause and effect cycle, you will default to an old idea and the cycle will default to an experience that was created before. That means the business will struggle, the weight will return, the relationship will fall apart, and so forth.

The Natural Experiential Cycle is creative. It is ongoing moment to moment. To the extent that you remain present and conscious when resistance shows up, you will be able to use those cycles to create both fulfilling experience and an expanding capacity to experience in ever more fulfilling ways. In the sense that I am using it here, "conscious" refers to knowing the guiding idea for the cycle you are in and not allowing a subversive idea to creep in by default, shifting you into a different creative cycle.

The results that you will have in terms of material outcomes are not the key. Expanding experience occurs through discovery. Lots of money, great relationships, good health, and much more are likely to be manifestations that occur at times during that discovery. Those physical manifestations are not the goal. They are just signs of discovery.

Summary

Who are you? You are energy. That energy organizes itself around ideas that resonate energetically. In other words, certain thoughts and things will resonate with your core energy and those thoughts and things are who you are in action or manifestation. The authentic you is the inspired you. It is the you that feels energized and alive.

Clarify who you are not as just an idea but as an idea becoming. The authentic you is naturally manifesting or becoming in the world. I call that process of becoming a Natural Experiential Cycle. The intention is not that you are becoming something final or complete. Rather, your becoming is an unlimited growing awareness. That Cycle is not created so that you can learn something new. It is created as the expansion of your awareness. Learning is a closed process that can be useful within a cycle. Awareness is an open process that brings forward altogether new cycles of discovery as experience expands and deepens naturally.

Finally, a Natural Experiential Cycle is an absolute cause and effect process of manifestation. Because it is natural, it can't be controlled, it can only be experienced. Depending upon the primary idea or who you think you are at any given time, that experience can either be expanding or limiting.

Clarifying *who you are* requires that you stay conscious especially when fear and resistance disrupt that natural flow of energy in a Natural Experiential Cycle. *Who you are* is the integration of idea, action, and learning. That integration takes the complete cycle and allows it to move into collective awareness so that you can know who you are in the larger sense of what energizes you. Start by *knowing* who you are. That knowing is an energetic knowing rather than logical or a conclusion. And from that knowing (energetic feeling), will come being and the clarity of a current idea of who you are. This clarity marks the first phase of the Cycle and it might be something like, "I am a very physically fit person."

If you say, "I am a rich person" and that idea comes from an energetic knowing that you love abundance in all its forms – spiritual, emotional, physical - then you will have started a Natural Experiential Cycle that will continue to provide you more and more of that abundance. If underneath that knowing or energetic connection, you have some logic which says that rich people are bad, then that *belief* will override the idea that *I am a rich person* and will instead substitute at a sub-conscious level something like, "I am a good person and good people don't have a lot of money and abundance." As your primary thought and belief, it will absolutely manifest in your Natural Experiential Cycles even though you think you want to be a rich person.

This process is not about right or wrong. It is a cause and effect process that is absolutely reliable. You get to choose whether who you are comes from what energizes you or from a logical concept of who you are. Your experience will result from that choice.

PART TWO

*Don't believe what your eyes are telling you. All they show
is limitation.
Look with your understanding, find out what you already
know, and you'll see the way to fly.*

Richard Bach

Resistance is any hesitation in the flow of a Natural
Experiential Cycle. Resistance is not the thing or person that
stands between you and what you want. It is the belief that
anything can stand between you and what you want. It can only
occur as the result of the belief that value - the ability to
experience - lies outside of you. When you have that belief, then
you also can resent those external things that seem to be in your
way.

For example, if you have an idea that really excites you and
you aren't moving into action, then you are in resistance. You
have the idea that something stands between you and what you
want and you are resisting the fact that it is there instead of doing
something about it. To illustrate this concept metaphorically,
picture a stream that is filled with rocks and boulders and so forth.
The water moves with purpose toward a destination somewhere in
the distance. Rocks and boulders block its way, but the water
simply moves around, under, over, and sometimes through the
various barriers. If the water went into resistance like humans do,
it would stop its flow and refuse to move forward because of the

69

rock that was in its way. Even though the water could move around it, it would stop and not only quit moving towards its destination, it would make a big deal about the rock being there in the first place.

It isn't what stands in your way and seems to resist you that keeps you from amazing experience. It is your *resistance* to what stands in your way. Working with resistance is being willing to move in those directions that are naturally inspiring to you without hesitating because of the various challenges, barriers, failures, and fears that you encounter along the way.

If you were to put your hand in a stream, you would find the water flexible and giving. You would not, however, want to mistake the softness of the water for a lack of direction and commitment. The water is influenced by many things, including your hand, but it is ruled only by the pull of gravity.

Suppose that you have an idea that inspires you and you feel resistance or fear about taking any action on the idea. Rather than trying to get rid of the feeling of resistance or fear, just allow those feelings and ask yourself how you can begin to let some kind of action occur anyway. That is the lesson of water. It stays in flow. The water does not change its mind about where it is going. Water is moved by an energy source (gravity) not logic (resistance to boulders). The water simply finds another path. The same is true for you when you are being authentically you. You might say that you are moved by *inspirational gravity*.

Inspirational gravity is the constant pull of those things that energize or inspire you. Like a river, you are pulled by that unchanging energy and your goal is to allow those rocks and boulders that stand in your path to influence how you move forward but never to become the *reason for your movement*. Humans sometimes change their mind about where they are going because of what stands in their way. To do that is to live an inauthentic life that is no longer guided by the energetic essence of inspirational gravity. That loss of inspirational pull is also the beginning of the appearance of chaos. Often, a clash of things in the material world that are pulled by gravity gives the appearance of chaos. But that clash of the physical does not scatter that which pulls. In the same way, failure and loss might confuse the logical mind but they cannot confuse your inspirational core. That ongoing internal energetic will bring a return to external order over time if you let it no matter how chaotic things might appear in the moment.

CHAPTER FOUR

RECOGNIZE THE
THREE POINTS OF RESISTANCE

*No pessimist ever discovered the secrets of the stars, or
sailed to an uncharted land, or opened a new heaven to the
human spirit.*

Helen Keller

The word resistance, in the way I am using it, suggests that
there is some kind of change occurring and, at the same time,
something causing disruption of the smooth flow of that process
of change. That disruption doesn't occur at random times but
rather it occurs at predictable times in the Natural Experiential
Cycle. It is during the most dramatic occurrences of change that
disruption is most likely to occur.

It can be useful to consider where in your life resistance tends
to show up most frequently so that you can be more proactive in
working with those challenges that are likely to occur.   That
conscious awareness can help you to stay in flow like a river so
that you can continue to be guided by your own inspirational
gravity rather than shifting into a cause against rocks and boulders.

You will tend to be more successful in leading a fulfilling life if you are willing to allow the challenges you encounter to change you. In other words, you don't really manage resistance from a place of inflexibility but rather you work with it from a place of willingness. Thus, change can be thought of as a co-creative process. It isn't a question of whether you will experience resistance. The only question is whether, in the midst of resistance, you will hold on to that which moves you while at the same time allowing flexibility in the journey.

Resistance Points

If the Natural Experiential Cycle is natural, then why don't you sit back and let it happen? Good question. The simple answer is probably fear. People are afraid that if they hold on to their bigger ideas, they will fail and experience some kind of pain. In my experience, I would say that you could expect instances of both failure and pain. Therefore, the logic for the resistance you feel is not necessarily faulty.

The illusion, however, is that if you choose something that seems safer, then you won't fail and experience some kind of pain. The assumption is that by avoiding pain you will experience pleasure or at least security. Experience tells me pain and failures are givens no matter what path you choose. Therefore, apart from not purposely hurting others or myself, I don't give pain undue thought.

As I said earlier, failure is a conditional judgment that occurs at the completion of a conceptual cycle. Since the higher-level outcome of the experiential cycle is awareness not winning, I don't worry about conditional judgments. I am more interested in the natural cycle and what it can do for me in terms of my experience. I want a steadily expanding experience.

Buddha said, "Suffering is holding on to pain." I don't like suffering so I try to leave my pain alone and let it go away by itself, which it always does. That, in essence, is how I manage pain. I let it go. As a result of the Natural Experiential Cycle, pain will go away – naturally. I sometimes need to affirm that natural cycle consciously in order to let go of an unconscious message that is telling me it could happen again.

Since there are three general phases in the cycle, then you might expect resistance to show up at those points where we are moving from one phase to the next. Those are the times of most dramatic change I referred to above. Let's take a look at the Natural Experiential Cycle in order to prepare for the resistance that is likely to occur as part of the process.

The first point of resistance is the transition from idea to action. If you have ever had an inspiring idea and kept it sitting in your head, then there is a good chance you are experiencing resistance to the natural transition from idea to action. Ask yourself this question: why would I not take action on an idea that inspires me? The answer is usually fear of something. Do you have an inspiring idea that you have put on hold?

The next point of resistance is the completion that occurs between action and learning. In our society, we have made completion a point of judgment, not just about an event but also about us personally. When an action is complete, we hand out grades or awards and sometimes, whether intentional or not, punishment. Completion can be a challenging place and sometimes the best thing to do seems to be to stay in action. Do you ever find that you have trouble completing things?

If you identify the goal of action to be winning or accomplishment, then you have set yourself up for getting stuck in a cycle. If you lose, you might hold on to the pain of the experience. And if you win, you might hold on to the pleasure of the experience. In either case, you delay experiential completion

75

and keep the experience from moving into your collective awareness.

If you identify the goal of action as the awareness that occurs as the result of completion, rather than the judgments and learning that occurs, then you set the stage for the experience to become valuable in a transformative way regardless of whether you win or lose. You place yourself in a situation where all of your experience contributes to ongoing inspiring ideas and you simply accept the pain that is an integral part of that expanding experience. The pain will pass with this approach and your experience will always be uplifting due to the nature of the source of your new ideas (collective awareness).

As a boy in high school and a young man in college, I was an avid football player until an injury ended my participation. I don't think there was ever a game that I played in that I didn't experience some level of pain. As a quarterback, I was the target of every person on the opposing team and part of their goal was to have me experience some kind of pain. I accepted that as part of the game and only rarely was I consciously aware of it. I loved the game and always looked forward to playing.

I also studied karate for a few years and remember my instructor talking about self-defense situations. During one class, he said that if anyone ever found themselves being attacked by someone with a knife, s/he should assume s/he would be stabbed or cut by the knife and focus on beating the other guy. In other words, in the case of both football and karate, it is important to accept some level of pain in order to effectively participate. Sometimes our fear of pain in business, relationships, and other everyday pursuits so dominates our thinking that we spend more time on ideas that will create that pain than those inspired ideas that can not only keep pain to a minimum but also bring us the joy we want. My experience is that when I have accepted pain as

76

part of the mix, I have only experienced it in minimal ways and it has always left by itself.

The final point of resistance is the letting go that occurs between learning and the collective awareness that births a new and inspiring idea. Your resistance can show up when it is time for a new idea and a new cycle. Holding on to the previous cycle, whether for good or bad reasons, will delay a new and expanded experience.

You might have to be somewhat disciplined with yourself when this resistance shows up. I say that because your mind will often fight very hard to hold on to concepts around an experience especially when that experience is extreme in any way. This letting go is the point in the cycle where rites of passage are typically practiced. The intention of a rite of passage is to help overcome any resistance to the new life level and the new ideas that will come from collective awareness.

In primitive societies such as that of the aborigines of Australia, for example, rites of passage were conducted in very serious and sometimes brutal ways. Letting go was considered to be critical to the growth and transformation of both individuals and society as a whole. In his book, *The Hero with a Thousand Faces*, Joseph Campbell discusses the nature of these rites:

> The so-called rites of passage, which occupy such a prominent place in the life of a primitive society (ceremonials of birth, naming, puberty, marriage, burial, etc.), are distinguished by formal, and usually very severe, exercises of severance, whereby the mind is radically cut away from the attitudes, attachments, and life patterns of the stage being left behind. [8]

This reference to primitive rites of passage suggests that personal expansion from one life level to another was understood to be a difficult process that required the help of the whole tribe. Those old attitudes, attachments, and life patterns did not go away easily. So it is with the challenge for you to let go of an old experiential cycle, especially if it was extreme in any way. Transformation from one life level to another can require severe exercises of severance or letting go.

This final point of resistance is, at its foundation, a resistance to experience itself. Experience is always new and changing. It is sometimes extreme. If you hold on to any particular phase of the cycle, then you are resisting change itself. If your experience has been good, you might hold on in order to avoid what might be bad or painful new experience. If your experience has been bad, then you might hold on in order to avoid a new experience, which is even worse, or so your logic may go -

Letting go is essentially submission to a collective awareness that has no boundaries or definition. I can't put into words the whole of my experience throughout time and space. I also can't put into words the nature of that experience integrated into the whole of all of the people and things that make up that collective awareness. I must simply trust that I will know in the most effective way possible through collective awareness as opposed to relying on past definitions and learning. The essence of collective awareness is creative energy and, as such, it is the creator of boundaries and definition, not a slave to them. By letting go then, I am giving power over my next idea to something that I don't understand or control. It is very hard for me to accept my collective awareness as being *understanding itself,* especially when pain is a requirement of understanding.

How do I let go of an idea that persists? I have found only one way. Earlier, I suggested an exercise where you tried not to look at anything red. Once that resonant idea of red has been planted in your conscious mind, it is difficult to let it go. As a result, you find yourself seeing everything red all around you. The only way to stop seeing red is to plant a different idea in your mind. So, for example, you let go of red by becoming conscious of blue or some other color or idea.

Often, however, we attempt to get rid of an unrewarding experience through logic. So for me, letting go of the pain of losing my wife, for example, would not have been helped by suggesting something logical like, "she is in a better place." Losing her and the pain associated with that experience was part of my life. Letting that pain occur and eventually pass happened by itself. It doesn't take logic to make it pass. And, in fact, logical attempts to explain why it happened or what is good about it can keep the pain present just like trying not to look at red keeps me seeing red everywhere I look.

So you might take a look at how fulfilling your experience is. In doing that, it might not be best to analyze the percentage of time that you are happy versus the percentage of time you are not. Winning and losing are not the issues.

Evaluating what your outcomes have been can be misleading and resonance that results from those failure-oriented outcomes might become founding ideas for your next cycle and a repeat of old experience. Instead, ask yourself how much resistance you feel in your life not from external things like boulders in a river, but in the flow of your own experience. Does your life feel like it flows in your career, your relationships, and your personal interests? Is it guided by inspirational gravity or an effort to eliminate barriers and boulders?

You don't manage your life. Your collective awareness and the cause and effect process of manifestation manage it. That awareness and process will produce the ideas that move you naturally into action. The only thing you manage is your own resistance to the challenges you encounter in your Natural Experiential Cycles.

Are you resisting the transition of your best ideas into action? That transition can be challenging. Be willing to be challenged without abandoning your own inspirational gravity. Are you resisting the completion of action? If so, then you are also resisting the learning that will occur with that completion, probably because it holds some kind of perceived pain for you. Are you resisting letting go of the learning (judgments and conclusions) about your old experience in order to make way for new and inspired ideas? If you are, don't be surprised by experience that tends to keep repeating itself in different ways.

The only thing you have to manage in this process is your own resistance. Those learned responses that hinder the letting go process are founded on the belief that conceptual cycles or learned responses are somehow true. Remember, conceptual cycles are only conditionally true and useful under specific conditions. That usefulness is always relative to an inspired idea but never the founder of that idea. The test for usefulness of learning is in its relationship with inspired ideas. Learning is always the servant of an inspired idea, and never its master. Learning that challenges an inspired idea is resistance. Learning that supports an inspired idea creates flow in the Natural Experiential Cycle and personal expansion.

When you work with resistance, you are choosing to trust the Natural Experiential Cycle. To put it differently, you are choosing to experience your life fully. When you submit to resistance, you are choosing to experience your life in a conditional and inauthentic way, always looking for guidance from the very rocks and boulders that get in your way.

Choosing to live life fully is not choosing pain or being masochistic. It is trusting that who you are at the level of collective awareness will choose ideas that produce the most exciting and motivating experience possible. Yes, you will experience pain, but you will keep your suffering to a minimum because you won't hold on to that pain.

Holding on to your best ideas will produce not only long-term results, but more importantly, it will produce immediate and ongoing results. It will do that because the source of your life will always be inspirational, meaning it will continually breathe life into you.

How does it feel when you are resisting a next step in the cycle? Let's consider the three potential resistance points: crisis of inspiration, challenge of action, and paradox of awareness.

Transition – The Crisis of Inspiration

Transition and the Crisis of Inspiration occur when an inspired idea begins to move into action. There is the potential for resistance at this point in the cycle.

When I was in my early twenties, I worked for someone on and off for several years while I was in college. I learned a great deal from him and from the experience of working various positions in his restaurants. There came a time, however, when the idea of opening my own restaurant occupied my thoughts more and more. My boss wanted me to stay with him, however, and didn't really support my inspired idea. That lack of support included ideas like maybe I wasn't ready, what about how good I had it, did I have enough money, etc.

It was true I had learned a lot with him and I was quite secure in how to do my job. I also had a circle of friends, credibility and some level of respect with co-workers, vendors, customers, and so forth. I felt that I was being pulled in two directions. I was experiencing that Crisis of Inspiration. If you look at figure 4 below, you can see graphically where the resistance was occurring. The arrow indicates the point of resistance to transition. I had an idea and I was resisting (with outside help, in this case) my natural desire to take action.

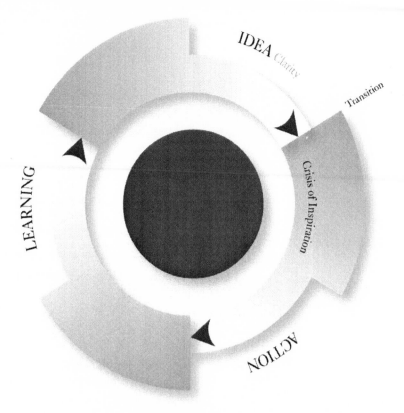

Figure 4

If you have ever had a really inspiring idea and gotten yourself upset because you couldn't decide what to do about it, you have experienced that Crisis of Inspiration. You have a certain comfort zone that relates to your known experience. You have created learning that allows you to be somewhat secure in the reliability of those conditional circumstances and you might choose that reliability and security over the creative experience that is always associated with ideas coming from the creative energetic that is collective awareness. Concern about self-esteem comes from the tests that we will surely undergo if we take action. If you see tests in the sense of outcome and performance, then self-esteem is, indeed, on the line. If you see tests as the requirement of engagement and experiential completion, then failure is not possible and personal expansion is assured.

A Crisis of Inspiration can lead to confusion and loss of clarity around your inspired idea. The reason is because you are resisting the natural flow of energy from idea to action. That resistance will cause your energy to back up and be concentrated in your mind. In other words, you can often end up putting your energy into an ongoing debate with yourself about what to do and never actually move into external action.

The behavior of electricity can provide an analogy that might help with this way of looking at self-leadership. Electricity is a kind of energy that most people use almost everyday. The electric current or energy starts at a source such as a battery, for example. The current then moves along a wire of some kind to a useful device such as a lamp and then it returns back to the source, in this case, the battery. That is called an electrical circuit.

Your Natural Experiential Cycle is much like that circuit. Energy comes from a source that inspires some idea in your mind. The energy then moves into action then to completion and the accompanying learning and then back to its source, which is collective awareness.

In an electrical circuit, the lamp used in the example above is sometimes called a resistor. It provides a measured amount of resistance that creates heat and the resulting light from the light bulb. What it doesn't do is stop the flow of energy. If that happens, you have what is sometimes called a "collected charge" which will stop the flow of energy and back up in the circuit and cause it not to work. The same is true in a Natural Experiential Cycle. If you have an inspired idea and don't take some kind of action, you may back up your own energy cycle. Over time, this can make you feel less alive and less connected.

In every area of your life, it is important to recognize when you are having a Crisis of Inspiration. If you allow it to go on too long without taking action, you are not working with resistance and that area of your life will suffer. Your goal in working with resistance when you are having a Crisis of Inspiration is to transition into action of some kind. What you are naturally inclined to do is being challenged (like rocks and boulders in a river) and you will want to manage that challenge with some kind of action.

Notice that in the analogy with electricity, resistance is how light is created in the light bulb. Your goal is to work with resistance, not to get rid of it. You are intending to experience new things and that requires a move from your comfort zone into what I call your discovery zone. In other words, you are moving outside of what you know and what feels comfortable.

If you are not at least a little uncomfortable in what you are doing, chances are you are not being moved by inspiration. There is a good chance that you are being moved more by fear and that you are seeking security. Security and personal expansion do not work well together.

Take a moment to reflect on the foundation for your choices in areas such as your career, relationships, personal fitness, and so forth. Are you choosing what to do based on what will seem to logically lead to an outcome designed for security? Or are you choosing what to do based on an idea that excites and moves you, and possibly makes you a little uncomfortable?

Then consider whether the actions you are currently taking reflect a desire for security or a desire for stimulation, excitement,

84

and personal expansion. Neither is right or wrong and the intention is not to create any judgment. It is simply to provide a way of looking at your motivating ideas so that you can consciously choose the direction you wish to take.

Working with your resistance is how you maintain personal expansion. Note that everyone has a different level of comfort and discovery. That means that just because someone else has taken a great risk, it doesn't mean that you should. Your goal is to recognize those ideas that inspire you and then move into taking action that is somewhat of a stretch for you. Comparing what others do with what you do can move you out of your own Natural Experiential Cycle and into a danger zone.

Completion – The Challenge of Action

The next point of resistance is completion or what I call the Challenge of Action. You can think of action as having purpose and that purpose is completion. Thus, the Challenge of Action is to move to completion. That might seem rather obvious, but people often resist completion. Why?

In our society, completion, as I said earlier, has become a place of judgment. Did you win or lose? What was your final grade or score? How well did you perform? All seem like useful questions especially, for example, if you are investing money in a business idea. The problem is that with that judgment can come fear. And fear can cause resistance in the natural cycle of personal expansion. Resistance can be useful in helping to determine how to do something, but not so useful if it challenges the original inspiring idea.

If you don't perform well, there can be pain. And, by not completing something, you won't have to experience the pain of judgment. Nor will you have to face the challenge of what to do next. Sometimes you just have it so good you don't want it to end.

When you were a child, your parents, teachers, coaches and others would get very excited when you won. They might not have gotten so excited when you lost. The idea was that if they supported great performance and discouraged poor performance, you would perform better and therefore have a more rewarding life.

The problem is that it doesn't necessarily work that way. One reason is probably because judgment can cause you to believe that value lies in something external. That kind of focus can keep you attached to a particular cycle, disallowing the integrated learning that comes from letting go.

My personal expansion principles are founded on the idea that the experiential cycle is natural. Natural here means that success is your nature rather than your goal. The idea that I need to learn how to be successful implies that something is missing from my basic nature. As a result, I will go looking for that learning and performance outside of myself in order to become whole and successful.

The Natural Experiential Cycle is founded on the idea that awareness, and its life-giving nature, is a natural process that accompanies natural experience. You don't make awareness happen, you let it happen. Your performance improves not because you try harder, but because you work with your own resistance to a natural process that is designed for expansion (and usually performance) simply by allowing yourself to move through it.

Figure 5 shows that the Challenge of Action resistance can occur at completion.

You have moved into action, but for any of a number of reasons (usually fear-based) you resist completion. Perhaps you have found that completion holds some kind of perceived penalty for you, which perhaps derives from childhood judgments around winning and losing. As the result of that resistance, lack of completion can become very frustrating. Along with the other resistance points, it can tend to keep people at a life level that becomes boring or dull because of the repeating experience.

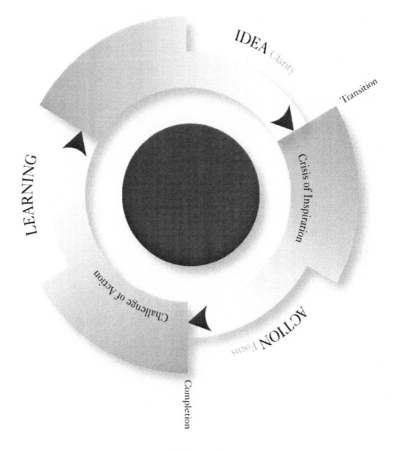

Figure 5

Your goal in working with resistance in the Challenge of Action phase is to move to completion. It can be extremely challenging to do that sometimes because you are moving to a place of judgment with which you might not be comfortable. Just remember that because of the cause and effect nature of the Natural Experiential Cycle, you are destined to repeat experiences that you are unable or unwilling to complete.

Letting Go – The Paradox of Awareness

The last point of resistance is letting go or what I call the Paradox of Awareness. It is the place where growth and transformation occur. The growth that occurs, however, does not happen in the way you might typically expect. You might think that gathering and holding on to more and more education is the key to growth and personal expansion. The paradox is, however, that it is only by letting go of that learning and allowing it to move into collective awareness that your capacity for awareness and personal expansion occurs. The paradox of learning is that you must let it go in order to experience personal expansion. There is an old Zen riddle that says: when you seek it, you can not find it. That riddle is referring to the paradox of learning. When you seek a lesson that will give you the big answer to life, you cannot find it. That is because the answer does not lie in conditional concepts; rather it lies in the nature of creative energy itself. The process of experience holds its own answers and so all you have to do is engage in the cycle and all is revealed through the experience itself. In other words, the answers you seek lie in the experience you are inspired to engage in, *not* in the result of that experience.

It seems to me that our educational system tends to make learning a linear process. In other words, learning has a clear goal that stems directly from what is taught. For example, in an MBA program, I will learn how to create a balance sheet for a business and how to read it. Then, when I open my business, I can create a balance sheet in exactly the way I was taught.

What our educational system doesn't teach is how to make that quantum leap in the imagination that takes us to a new life level or a new business level. In Timothy Ferris's book *Coming of Age in the Milky Way*, a quantum leap is described as follows.

When a photon strikes an atom, boosting an electron into a higher orbit, the electron moves from the lower to the upper orbit instantaneously, without having traversed the intervening space. . . the electron simply ceases to exist at one point, simultaneously appearing at another. [9]

That quantum leap is not a linear process. The electron does not traverse the intervening space. I am suggesting that in the same way an electron makes a quantum leap, so too do you make a quantum leap in imagination when you let go of judgments and conclusions including educational lessons.

The current educational approach to learning seems to imply that if you learn your lessons well, you will be able to live a happy and rewarding life. It stops short of the real value of education, which lies in the integration of knowledge and learning in collective awareness. It is in collective awareness that your creative energy can give birth to a brand new idea. You don't need to go to school to become aware. You only need to participate in your own experience.

Knowing how to read a balance sheet probably won't be the key that takes my business to a new level. That isn't to say it isn't useful. Its usefulness, however, is limited to a pre-defined need and solution. In other words, it is useful in an existing process but unlike collective awareness, it won't provide the imaginative results that are required for a leap to something completely new. Lessons are great for use under limited conditions; but without integration through a process of letting go, they cannot contribute in a way that is unlimited.

For example, one moment you are not a businessman or woman and the next moment you are. There is no time or space to traverse between what you were and what you are now. The only thing that is needed is your inspired idea, which comes to you much like the photon striking the atom in quantum physics. The idea itself works on you in a non-linear, multidimensional way that transforms you in ways you cannot foresee. It is a change that emanates from an unknown source. And that unknown source is not unknown because it is not familiar, but because it is the creator of definition and not the result of it. That unknown source is the creative energy of collective awareness and it cannot be defined because it is not the extension of any one idea or concept. It is the source of ideas, not the extension of them.

We tend to exhibit two kinds of change. One is linear and happens within a process or cycle. And the other is non-linear and quantum and seems to happen almost magically, like the change from a caterpillar to a butterfly. Timothy Ferris discusses the idea of quantum theory, which was developed by Max Planck around 1900, in his book *Coming of Age in the Milky Way*. He says " – only if he [Planck] abandoned the classical assumption that energy is emitted continuously and replaced it with the unprecedented hypothesis that energy comes in discrete units. Planck called these units quanta . . ." [10] When I refer to quantum change, I am suggesting that the new idea is not an extension of an old idea but is a discrete unit without any clear connection to what came before.

The first or linear kind of change is managed at some level of consciousness and the other, non-linear kind of change occurs at the unconscious level of collective awareness. As a result, your job in making that leap is essentially getting out of the way of your natural experiential cycle. That transformative leap in imagination happens after completion of action and its resulting learning.

I call it the Paradox of Awareness because the way that you allow that jump to a new idea is by letting go of a consciousness that is cycle bound. We don't become more aware along a linear path by trying to become more aware. We become more aware by letting go of that old experience and letting it work at an unconscious level with all of our other experiences and everything around us. That is not always easy and it doesn't come from the logical mind that is often trained in school.

Maybe you know of someone who had some kind of success in the past and is still holding on to it. That old success comes up in conversation over and over again and maybe the person actively keeps material reminders of it in a way that might seem excessive. There may appear to be a lot of busy-ness in his/her relationships or at work, but not a lot of change and personal expansion.

That is an example of the Paradox of Awareness. The more someone holds on to an old learning in the form of conclusions or judgments, the more someone keeps themselves at that old life level. And the more they stay at that old level, the duller his or her experience can become regardless of how busy they might appear. In fact, you might wonder if all that busy-ness is a sign of a mind that is filled with ideas battling against each other as the result of energy that is backed up due to resistance.

Another example of the Paradox of Awareness is holding on to an old experience that was very painful or even traumatic. Again, the way to the new life level is through completion, learning, and letting go. The way out is not a conscious process, although the way to the door out can be.

In the business world, people will hold on to an old idea because it worked at sometime in the past. The general rule in this regard is if something is working, then keep doing it. Likewise, in everyday life, many people today get married and hold on to being single. Many people move into adulthood and still act as children. It is neither right nor wrong that they do this. It is simply a choice

91

and it can prevent their transformation or quantum leap in personal expansion. It takes some courage to let go. Like the old Lakota Indian saying goes, when you find yourself sitting on a dead horse, dismount.

Sometimes it can be useful to engage in a specific activity, such as a ritual or celebration, to help you let go. We still celebrate rites of passage in our culture but not always in the way they were intended. A rite of passage is intended to signify completion of something like childhood or being single and opens the door to a new life level. That completion is not meant to be vague. It is meant to be absolute.

As you begin to build a business, for example, you will go through many different cycles at many different levels of the business. The primary cycle is the complete business life cycle from opening to selling or closing the business, possibly lasting many years. You will have smaller cycles such as creating and selling your first product or breaking even in sales.

The end of these cycles can be celebrated in a way that opens the door for the next phase of the business. Those celebrations can be fun or somber depending upon the nature of the event celebrated. In any case, it can be useful to be aware of any resistance to letting go that either delays completion or inhibits acknowledgement of that completion in a celebration. If you sense that resistance, it can be useful to work with it as best you can by letting go in order to support both your own natural transformation and the transformation of what you seek to create. These same principles apply to relationships, personal fitness and so forth.

Figure 6 illustrates the point in the Natural Experiential Cycle where the Paradox of Awareness occurs. With the completion of action, you will gain learning. With the willingness to let go comes personal expansion and inspired new ideas.

You can think of this third point of resistance as resistance to letting go. Letting go allows you to be present to collective awareness and its inspiration. One way to look at the idea of letting go is to understand the concept of mindfulness.

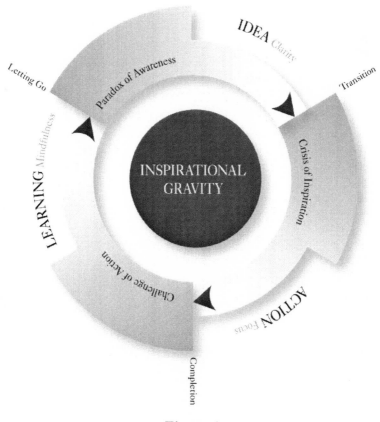

Figure 6

Ven. Henepola Gunaratan, a Buddhist monk describes mindfulness as follows.

> When you first become aware of something, there is a fleeting instant of pure awareness just before you conceptualize the thing, before you identify it. That is a stage of Mindfulness. Ordinarily, this stage is very short. It is that flashing split second just as you focus your eyes on the thing, just as you focus your mind on the thing, just before you objectify it, clamp down on it mentally and segregate it from the rest of existence. It takes place just before you start thinking about it--before your mind says, "Oh, it's a dog." That flowing, soft-focused moment of pure awareness is Mindfulness. In that brief flashing mind-moment you experience a thing as an un-thing. You experience a softly flowing moment of pure experience that is interlocked with the rest of reality, not separate from it. [11]

If you are holding on to conceptualizations from a previous cycle, then you will get extensions of those concepts rather than inspiration from collective awareness. In other words, you will repeat the cycle in some way. Mindfulness occurs when you are able to let go of those concepts and conclusions. Notice that the center of the cycle is Inspirational Gravity. That is what powers the whole cycle and it is essential to stay connected to that life giving creative energy by letting go.

Dr. Jon Kabat-Zinn, founder and former Executive Director of the Center for Mindfulness in Medicine, Health Care, and Society at the University of Massachusetts Medical School describes mindfulness as follows.

> Mindfulness is about being fully awake in our lives. It is about perceiving the exquisite vividness of each moment.

We feel more alive. We also gain immediate access to our own powerful inner resources for insight, transformation, and healing. [12]

Mindfulness is allowing all of the pieces of the cycle and thoughts about it to become the one experience that moves into the unconscious collective awareness so that you can remain present and connected to your energetic essence or collective awareness. It is in that unknown zone of the unconscious where transformation occurs.

If you took a chance in the past and were successful, you might be afraid to try something new and give up the idea upon which that success is founded. The problem is that the good experience lies in the past and it might not be enough to just live in old memories. People sometimes resist their own experience. They collect ideas of other peoples' experience or memories of their own past experience instead of seeking their own next journey. For example, our national devotion to television could be seen as making us more like butterfly collectors (as in Stafford's poem at the beginning of Chapter Two) because the act of watching TV causes us to engage in a less authentic (second hand) experience.

R. H. Macy, founder of Macys department store, had to let go of at least five failures before he finally opened his first successful store in Manhattan. Abraham Lincoln had to let go of many election defeats before he finally won the election that would put him in the White House. We often admire those people who experience great challenges and are able to move on in spite of the pain of a failure or loss. We recognize in them that essential nature that is transformed through endings and is not defeated by them.

The failures they experienced included all kinds of pain. I would also guess that all of these people experienced some level of resistance when they tried to let go and open up to new ideas.

95

However, they were able to work with that resistance by allowing the Natural Experiential Cycle to be the basis for their motivation instead of ideas about winning and losing, pleasure and pain.

Learn to recognize resistance to letting go. In some cases, such as a traumatic experience, that process of letting go can take longer. The process of completing an experience and letting it go experientially works along a natural timeline that can't really be predicted or controlled. Allow it to be a natural process. If, however, you find that you are in some way holding on to what is naturally changing and ending, then you might want to consider that you are resisting. You will experience pain, but you don't have to suffer.

If you can let go, you can then allow yourself to quietly discover what lies next. Recognize when you are in resistance. That is where the real work of personal expansion takes place in your relationships, career, and all other areas of your life. It is through that integrating of completed experience that the quantum leap in ideas can take you to a new level of life.

As you read this book, I'm guessing that you are thinking about those ideas that inspire you. Those are your best ideas because they come from collective awareness and have the ability to transform your experience. That is a good thing not because these ideas guarantee a particular outcome, but because they guarantee a full, life-giving experience. If, for example, you are an entrepreneur, you may or may not get rich, but by engaging, you will expand your experience in ways you can't now imagine.

If you haven't already taken action on those ideas that inspire you then you might ask yourself why you are resisting what is your Natural Experiential Cycle. The intention of that question is to help you work with your resistance so that you can move into action as soon as possible.

Notice I am saying you want to work with your resistance. You don't want to eliminate it because without it you will ultimately miss the opportunity for the cycle to add significant experience to collective awareness. In other words, if your experiential cycles are too easy, then the experience can have a minimal impact.

As described earlier, you can think of this cycle as being like an electrical circuit where the wiring must go from a source to a device like a lamp and then return to the source. If you look at the wire connected to a lamp, you will see two wires not one. One wire carries the electricity to the lamp and the other carries the electricity back to the source. Without that complete circuit, the lamp won't create any light. You might also note that the reason the lamp creates light is that the light bulb creates resistance to the electricity. That resistance appears in the form of light and heat energy. Having a circuit with no resistance is essentially useless. In the same way, if the light bulb creates too much resistance, then it will stop the flow of electricity.

The situation in the Natural Experiential Cycle is analogous. The flow of energy from your source, or creative energy, appears as an idea that wants to transition into action. Some level of resistance is likely to be experienced at this transition point. You will want to work with the resistance in a way that gets you into action in the most effective way possible: that is, in the way that can also allow your energy to flow.

For one person, the ideas and action might be much more aggressive than for another. While competition can be both fun and useful, it is important to understand how it can be useful. It makes sense to compete with others who are at similar or slightly higher levels than you. That type of competition can help you break through self-limiting beliefs. Those breakthroughs occur because in the competition, those you are competing with inspire your performance to some extent. It is not unlike letting go of your own judgments and allowing collective awareness to provide a new idea of who you are. In this case, your competitors are providing that new and inspiring idea as the result of their performance. You let go by allowing yourself to compete regardless of winning or losing.

I once observed a high level manager move her team to completion in order to set the stage for a higher level of awareness in the next cycle. She worked in a high tech environment managing a team of software developers. They had created an upgraded version of an existing program and set a time to upload the program to replace the older version. Due to the nature of the business, the computer system could not be shut down or it would have worldwide impact that would hurt the company and customers as a result. So there was a great deal of pressure to get the job done right and to get it done quickly.

The director set a time to meet at night in order to minimize the impact of the process on the worldwide network. The team met at the appointed time and the director gave the go-ahead to begin the upload. A variety of small problems began to surface and after a short time, the upgrade was still not on track.

The director called a halt to the process and declared the effort complete. She told everyone to button up the system with the old version in place and said that she was going across the street to have a beer and a burger. She said she was buying and invited anyone who cared to come to join her. Everyone went and spent the time in a relaxed social get-together.

The project was not conceptually complete, but she made it experientially complete by declaring it so and then supporting her team in a way that helped each of them complete their own Natural Experiential Cycles. The next day, she had the team review the process, make changes, and meet again that night for another try. The upload went without a hitch and the new software version was successfully in place.

Notice that this director was not ruled by the concept of completion. Rather, she was sensitive to the experiential cycle and her ability to control it by simply declaring the cycle complete. Furthermore, she completely let go of the failure to install and managed her team in a way that encouraged them to let go as well. The process she used - going out for a beer and hamburger - could be compared to a ritual or celebration of completion. This is an excellent example of managing resistance to completion. She was and is a hard driving goal-oriented person. She recognized Natural Experiential Cycles and managed the resistance that showed up in this particular cycle exceptionally well.

Completion and the learning that accompanies it is the goal of action and you will want to manage resistance to it or you can leave yourself stuck in non-productive action. If this director had insisted on completion on the first night, she might have kept her team in an unproductive action that could have caused significant problems for the company. Equally as important, she created a ritual or celebration to help everyone let go of what could have been labeled a failure. Her team let go of the experience, integrated it and set the stage for the expansion needed to complete the job in a successful way the next night.

Be sensitive to your own experiential cycles and manage your own resistance to completion. Once you have completed action, you will have a new outcome and learning. You will want to let go of that result or outcome completely in order to let the experience move into your collective awareness. It cannot go there until and unless you let go of the specific conceptual expectation regardless of whether you judge that result good or bad. Once you let go of expectation, you can then effectively work with resistance in experiential cycles.

In other words, you must recognize that when you let go of a particular conclusion, you are not letting go of the larger experience. However if you don't let it go, then you will be keeping it in a form that will not allow it to integrate with all of your experience and become optimally useful. This conceptual form will interfere with the revelation of that new idea that is the inspiration of your collective awareness and the foundation for your new experience.

New ideas based on fear

Suppose that you have the idea of starting a new relationship or business. I use those two ideas because I have experienced both in challenging ways. I lost my wife of 23 years to cancer and I lost two businesses that I had built over 14 years to an economic crash.

I experienced a great deal of fear about starting a new relationship because of the intense pain I felt when my wife died. I wasn't sure I wanted to take a chance that such pain could happen again. I also felt fearful about starting a new business. What if I put in years of work again and then lost it all because of another economic failure of some kind? Could I trust my own ideas regarding a new relationship or business?

It is not unusual to feel fear when you have an idea that in the past resulted in a painful experience. How can you manage resistance to an idea that comes from collective awareness and brings up fear? The answer is to trust the idea and work with the fear and resistance.

The idea of committing to a relationship or starting a business can be a naturally occurring phase in your creative cycle. You can't control what is natural. So, I don't spend time thinking about whether I should have a new relationship. And I don't spend time thinking about whether I should have a new business. If the idea comes to me in a natural and inspiring way from my collective awareness, then it is right for me.

The challenge has to do with the danger of replacing that natural idea with an idea that can keep me creating from an old unrewarding cycle. So, if I allow my fear to create the new idea, then it will be attached to that part of my relationship with my wife that was painful. In other words, I will define my 23-year relationship with my wife based on a single event that was painful. What about all of that time with her that was rewarding?

My collective awareness includes all of that time and my conclusions and judgments about the painful parting include little or none of that rewarding time. Collective awareness says do it again. Conditional conclusions say don't do it again.

Managing resistance to an idea does not mean that the new idea will be exactly like the old one. To the extent that I am able to stay present and conscious, the new idea will include the best of the old experience with new discoveries happening all the time. I am a creative being and if I support that creativity, it will happen naturally. I don't have to be particularly smart or talented. I am creative by nature, not by learning.

Holding the idea of building a new business doesn't mean that I will run the business exactly as I did my old one. The Natural Experiential Cycle will naturally produce a new idea from collective awareness that is fresh and evolved without trying. I will be more aware of economic issues and their potential impact on my new business. I only have to stay present and everything that I need to know and do will happen naturally.

Opening that new business isn't inviting the same outcome unless I allow my new idea to come from fear. If it comes from collective awareness, it will also be coming from an expanding awareness and a consciousness that is growing in its ability to be present. That natural cycle doesn't eliminate pain. It is expansive and creative and it comes from the best that I have to bring to my life. Pain shifts from something to be avoided to something that gives breadth and depth to my experience and my collective awareness.

The feel of resistance

Staying conscious is a key to grounding the life that inspires you. It is what makes managing resistance possible. Since the creative process is a moment-by-moment experience, you will want to be present on a moment-to-moment basis. That presence isn't designed to keep you in charge. It is designed to keep you aware.

Think of a recent encounter you had with someone. It can be anyone - a significant other, boss, child, or whoever. Take the position of an observer in the encounter: you are a fly on the wall in your own interactions.

Now remind yourself that you are creative by nature and were creating something in this encounter. Observe how your creative process influenced the interaction in order to accomplish something. If you are a creative being, then every interaction is creative. There are no encounters where creativity is not at work. Chatting by the water cooler is not a break from creativity. It is just a different kind of creativity.

What was the role you created for yourself? Did you notice any time when you were not conscious and you were just running an old program? In other words, can you notice times when you let go of a higher goal or inspired idea and just defaulted to an old fear-based idea to run the conversation? Maybe your higher goal in this case was simply to get to know someone new.

The goal here is not to judge how well you did. You are creating right now as you read this book, so if you draw any conclusions or judgments, you are setting yourself up for your next creative cycles that could be based on fear. You goal here is observation. You want to see how you created that interaction, not why you created it.

As you see how you create, you might well have a thought about how you are going to create next time. You can also identify how a thought came to you in the interaction and you resisted it. What did you say and what didn't you say? Notice how you created the experience for yourself by making those choices. Was that the experience you wanted? Did you resist some kind of natural knowing that was occurring in the exchange? Did you manage your end of the conversation in a way that protected you or in a way that expanded you?

You don't work with resistance by judging it. You work with it first by identifying it. You will want to feel resistance in the moment, for it is only in that moment that resistance can be managed. You can't manage what you say to someone after the conversation is over. You can't work with what you aren't aware of. You must be consciously aware and that means aware of the feeling of resistance as it happens.

That conscious awareness will allow a new idea and that new idea will produce a new action perhaps in the form of saying something that you were resisting. It is sometimes said that awareness is often self-curative. That means that simply being aware of destructive behavior can cause you to think and act differently. It also implies that you might be unaware of why you do much of what you do. If you are not conscious of resistance in the moment, then default ideas will tend to run the conversation. You will say what you have always said and you will create the experience that you have always created.

Resistance is like a red flag. Become aware of that feeling of resistance because it is trying to tell you something. It is trying to tell you that you might be getting ready to repeat an old belief. At that moment, you will want to go conscious and assess what is going on. Think of the feeling of resistance as a question. Do you want to default to old patterns or will you allow the birth of a new experience or new discovery that is trying to naturally occur?

Make the choice in the moment to create new or old experience. There is no right or wrong. However, this is the

103

moment in time where you make a decision to ground the life that inspires you or to let that life-giving idea die. Inspired ideas that do not transition into action can leave you in what has been called the Waste Land. The Waste Land is that place where a loss of meaning in life occurs. No one there has the courage to live an authentic life: and instead, a Waste-Lander lives according to what others do or tell him/her to do. T. S. Eliot's poem, *The Waste Land*, describes this place of loss of meaning.

In the *Hero with a Thousand Faces*, Joseph Campbell retells a story, by Wolfram von Eschenbach, that illustrates the moment in time when resistance can make or break you where discovery and personal expansion are concerned. The narrative concerns Parzival, a knight in King Arthur's court, which I summarize in the following paragraphs.

Parzival, who has undergone many trials in the process of questing, comes upon a pond where the Grail King is fishing. The Grail King represents the self that has lost its connection to what is natural and authentic within each person. As a result of this loss of connection, the King and all of the people in his kingdom are under a spell. This spell has them all trapped in the Waste Land and the only way to break the spell is through the *spontaneous act of a noble heart*, i.e. compassion. The Waste Land is that place where people behave in a calculating and self-centered way rather than being present to those ideas that naturally come up in the course of experience especially with regard to compassion.

As a knight, Parzival has been taught to be courteous, chivalrous, courageous, and to do other knightly things and so the stage is set for him to break the spell over the kingdom. However, he is not aware of the spell. This is a good thing because only someone who is not aware of the spell can break it. If that person is aware of the spell, then his actions won't be spontaneous.

Parzival asks the King if he knows of a place where he might stay for the night. The King and those in the kingdom know that the spell can only be broken by the spontaneous act of compassion. Seeing Parzival, the King thinks that maybe this is the man who can perform that compassionate act so he tells Parzival how to get to the castle.

A great feast is prepared and everyone in the castle is filled with the anticipation that the spell will finally be broken. Parzival is seated for the great feast and the King is brought in: he looks ill and unable to walk. This is the moment where Parzival is confronted with his own natural instincts versus an old idea of how he should act.

As a knight, he was taught not to ask questions of a personal nature to strangers. Yet, his natural impulse is to show the compassion that he is feeling for the King and ask him what is wrong. Unfortunately, in this case, Parzival chooses to be guided by an old idea of what he should do as a knight instead of allowing compassion to move him to ask the spell-breaking question.

The opportunity for the spontaneous act of a noble heart passes and everyone sighs in great disappointment knowing that the spell will not be broken that night. They all go to bed very unhappy and Parzival has no idea what has happened.

Like Parzival, you have the choice to be guided by either the natural creative cycle or an old idea. The key is coming to recognize when resistance is happening in the moment. It is the warning that a choice is being made. If you are present, your choices will not be made by default, as Parzival's were, and you can support your own natural process of creating experience that is expansive and fulfilling. If you feel that you are "under a spell" in some area of your life, you might become an observer of how you create those same experiences over and over. You might also recognize that breaking the spell will require the spontaneous act of your noble heart.

CHAPTER FIVE

BE WILLING TO BE CHANGED

*The significant problems we face today cannot be solved at
the same level of thinking we were at when we created them.*
Albert Einstein

There are two ways of looking at change that can be useful
here. One is a change in goals and the other is a change in
methods. For example, assume that you had planned a trip to
Paris and made reservations on a plane to get there from the U. S.
The goal is Paris and the method is air travel. One type of change
you could make would be to change the goal or destination to
Hawaii instead. Another type of change you could make would be
to change the method but keep the original goal. So you might
cancel the flight reservations and instead go by boat to France and
then train to Paris.

Understanding the difference can be important in working
with resistance. You have certain ideas that inspire or breathe life
into you. Those ideas represent your inspirational gravity or that
which moves you. You don't really have a lot of choice about that.
Certain things move and excite you and others don't. That
"destination mechanism" like the gravity that pulls water is not

subject to much change, at least not from a mental or intellectual standpoint.

The method or journey that results from that inspirational pull, however, is the very nature of change. Being willing to be changed is really being willing to experience or discover the life that is created as the result of your inspiration co-creating in the world as you find it each day.

Being willing to be changed isn't compromising on your goal or that which breathes life into you. It is being willing to experience the journey of that inspiration as one of discovery rather than experiencing that journey as a job or sacrifice required in order to have what you want.

Change is natural

The idea that change is natural is more than just stating that change is going to happen in some potentially random fashion. Natural means that the way change occurs not only has purpose but (more accurately), is purpose itself. Change is neither chaotic nor organized. It is a process. It is whole and the language that attempts to view its parts creates the illusion that it is not. Change is always purposeful even though it might appear chaotic to us at some point in time.

Change has been described in many ways in mythology and science. In mythology it is understood as a process of renewal or creation. Science has had a more difficult time with it because of the attempt to divide it into parts. When looked at from this perspective, it appears as a paradox. In her book, *Leadership and the New Science*, Margaret Wheatley writes:

> When we concentrate on individual moments or fragments of experience, we see only chaos. But if we stand

back and look at what is taking shape, we see order. Order always displays itself as patterns that develop over time.

In much of new science, we are challenged by paradoxical concepts – matter that is immaterial, disequilibrium that leads to stability, and now chaos that is ordered. Yet the paradox of chaos and order is not new. As ancient myths and new science both teach, every system that seeks to stay alive must hold within it the potential for chaos, . . . It is chaos' great destructive energy that dissolves the past and gives us the gift of a new future. It releases us from the imprisoning patterns of the past by offering us its wild ride into newness. Only chaos creates the abyss in which we can recreate ourselves. [13]

Thus, change is natural, which means that it has its own in-built control mechanisms. Those control mechanisms are inherent in change, not something that we must provide through intellectual control. On the contrary, it is the attempt at intellectual control of change that creates resistance to it and disrupts the natural process of energetic renewal.

Change is not change from this to that. Thinking about it in those terms suggests an attempt to conceptualize experience and dissect it into parts. Change is a whole that manifests over time. All aspects of change are creative and no single aspect of change is the source of change. The source is creative energy and it is natural or inherent to the whole.

It is not easy to be in the midst of what feels like chaos. Fear frequently accompanies that experience and our response is often to attempt intellectual control in order to stay safe and preserve ourselves. While I support the effort to be safe, it is important to consider what it is that you are trying to protect.

If you are trying to hold on to old structures, ideas, routines, and so forth that are no longer working, then it is some aspect of ego that is being protected. Letting that go is moving into chaos of some type and it is change naturally doing its thing. It is the way to the new you and for that new you to emerge, you must let it all go into your collective awareness.

Change occurs in the Natural Experiential Cycle through transition, completion, and letting go. Those three points of resistance are the points where the life that inspires you is grounded. They are the points where experience, whether thrilling and enjoyable or chaotic and frightening, becomes real.

You can't control what is natural

The nature of a Natural Experiential Cycle is inherent to the cycle as a whole. The first phase of the cycle is an idea or information. That idea or information is not the source of the cycle; rather it is part of the cycle. The cycle is creative, with the source of that creativity inherent to all phases of the cycle. That means that ideas and information are not the source of creativity: they are part of it.

So, you do not create as the result of your intellect or thinking. Rather, your thinking is creativity itself. This brings up the issue of control. Do you have any control in a system that is natural? The answer is no. A system that has a natural control mechanism built in cannot be controlled; it can only be resisted. To resist it from the standpoint of controlling it is an exercise in futility. Efforts to control it will often manifest as a new cycle based on fear and focused solely on gaining control. To participate in the cycle from the standpoint of influence rather than control holds on to the inspired basis for the cycle and it is how you manage or work with resistance. No matter how smart or crafty or intellectually adept you are, you cannot use that intellect to gain control over creative energy and the ideas it produces. The attempt to do so creates the illusion that ideas and information are not experience itself.

The old question, "would you rather be right or happy?" refers to this illusion. If you think that an idea is not an experience, you can hold on to that idea even though it makes you unhappy. In other words, you can be right. You would only do that if you thought that your ideas weren't experience but instead accurately *represented* experience. They don't. They are creative and what they are creating is experience. Your life is one of creative experience and you can either participate in the experience in a way that is expanding or you can participate in a way that is contracting.

Expanding experience is deeply rewarding and fulfilling. It can happen when you work with resistance in a way that influences creative energy at those three points of resistance. That influence is the creative act manifesting. Contracting experience is more like the Waste Land Parzival encounters: that is, a place of resisting the idea that something is naturally influencing you. That can happen when, instead of working with resistance, you attempt to eliminate it by controlling whatever seems to be causing it. Responding to resistance with an effort to control typically shifts you out of your original inspiring idea and into an idea focused on external control rather than personal expansion. You disconnect from the very thing that breathes life into you. Parzival attempted to control the King's influence on him by doing the "right" thing rather than the authentic thing.

Don't try to think yourself to happiness and success by being right. To do so is to resist what is a natural process of expansion. Instead, work with your resistance to internal and external challenges, especially during times of chaos, by influencing and allowing yourself to be influenced by what is a creative process. That kind of interactive influence is what I call "optimal influence." It is how you work with resistance to the things that

111

seem to stand in your way. In order to bring about the change of personal expansion, you will use the process of optimal influence by both influencing things externally and allowing yourself to be influenced at the same time. Demanding the one while resisting the other denies the dynamics of change. The world around you cannot change if you aren't willing to change with it. When you use optimal influence, you will participate in that creative process rather than attempting to control it from a safe and unchanging place.

Be willing to discover your natural self

Sometimes challenges come up where I can't seem to find a good choice or solution for what to do next. If I can't find a solution that seems good enough, I might resist moving forward. I might remain where I am in the cycle and be unable to move in some way. Rather than choosing to be happy, I choose to be right.

In November of 1998, my lovely, green-eyed, blonde wife died of cancer. For those who have experienced such loss, it might be possible to identify with the emptiness that I felt and the desire to hold on to the more than 23 wonderful years we had together. My expectation before losing her was for a natural cycle that would last many more years and include grandchildren, travel and so forth.

Built into all of those dreams was the idea that I would share them with my wife. Without her, the structure of those expectations fell apart. It isn't really possible to put into words what that kind of loss feels like. One must experience it to know.

One thing was clear much as I resisted it. Completion had occurred with her death. I could not find a good choice or solution that would change what was absolutely complete. And yet it took years for me to experientially catch up to that fact. Much of the resistance to that letting go seemed to lie at a subconscious level. Conscious new choices helped to let go of that experiential cycle. For example, I moved to a new town, became very active in a personal growth program, and started socializing with people I hadn't known before.

It is often hard to be willing to accept what is complete. It might be losing a race or a business, or dealing with the results of a poor life-choice. Or it might be surviving a significant personal loss or illness. We sometimes resist those unwanted life occurrences in very persistent ways because we feel very much out of control.

When you find yourself in resistance, how can you best work with it? The answer is to adopt an attitude of willingness – willingness to both exercise influence in the event to the extent you can and to be influenced by that event. An attitude of willingness allows you to move through the natural experiential cycle thus allowing both experiential integration and personal transformation to occur. The essence of willingness is letting go of whatever security you feel in that old incomplete cycle and accepting the creative role of optimal influence rather than seeking control.

In The Hero with a Thousand Faces, Joseph Campbell says:

> The myths and folk tales of the whole world make clear that the refusal is essentially a refusal to give up what one takes to be one's own interest. The future is regarded not in terms of an unremitting series of deaths and births, but as though one's present system of ideals, virtues, goals, and advantages were to be fixed and made secure. [14]

Campbell demonstrates that the issue of resistance is not new or relegated to any one time in history or any one group of people. Resisting at any of the three points I outline in the Natural Experiential Cycle is dealing with the uncomfortable part of the creative process. It challenges your comfort zone and, like it or not, moves you into your discovery zone. Those three points of resistance are also the places where you feel most alive.

Discovering your natural self is a natural process governed by your core nature, not your logical mind. That natural self is not a concept but a lifetime of experience. It is not a final knowing but rather, an ongoing knowing once you have connected with your core energy. It is not a conceptual knowing but an energetic knowing that can only occur when you are connected with creative energy.

Everyone I know has a dream of some kind. I have a friend who was a homeless woman for a number of years. She had experienced things like spousal abuse, cancer, and other difficult challenges. As a homeless woman, she had a dream of creating beautiful art that represented her loving nature and she is taking action today to make that dream a reality. That woman has remembered who she is not as a concept, but as an energy that she can feel. We all have those dreams because it is our nature to have them.

She had painted beautiful somewhat abstract flowers on scraps of paper, pieces of cardboard, or almost anything else that provided her with a small canvas. And she did so in a style that expressed her loving nature. When I saw them and felt her energy, I suggested she take them to a printer to make them available to more people. I helped her create a name for her new company, a simple logo, and a tagline that represented her passion. The printer was very helpful and gave her great discounts and free services to make her paintings into greeting cards and prints. A paper supplier donated some of the paper for printing. The result is a dream she achieved despite the obvious resistance a homeless person might feel to turning a dream into reality.

Allowing those inspired and energizing ideas to take form in the real world is often a daunting task. And you have probably lived long enough to have taken action on at least one inspired idea only to have it crushed in the real world the moment you started to do something about it. Those inspired ideas by their nature are the expansion of your energy. The word inspire means *to breathe life into* and those great ideas do exactly that. But the real world sometimes seems to take the life out of them and in so doing, seems to take the life out of you.

You must always bear in mind, however, that renewal and regeneration come naturally by moving through the cycle to mindfulness and transformation. That mindfulness relates to the just completed cycle and it can occur by taking a vacation, sleeping deeply, or even just taking a walk. With that letting go, you can return to that internal place that cannot be crushed by external events.

A willingness to discover your natural self starts with the connection to your own internal energy or inspirational gravity. That energy does not move according to logical concepts or thinking. Rather, logical concepts and thinking are created out of that internal energy. The ideas that are created out of that energy source will stir you to action as naturally as the creation of the ideas themselves. The natural result of those actions will be new learning as the experiential cycle is completed. And the natural result of that integrated learning and the cycle that produced it is the birth of a new idea that is energetically who you are in the present. In the words of William James, "I have often thought that the best way to define a man's character would be to seek out that particular mental or moral attitude in which, when it came upon him, he felt himself most deeply and intensely active and alive. At such moments there is a voice inside which speaks and says: This is the real me!" [15]

Your Natural Experiential Cycles are cycles of manifestation. They are the energy that is yours to experience. Discovering your natural self simply requires your willingness to experience all that is revealed in a Natural Experiential Cycle. With the completion of each cycle you might say you are filled up. Preparing for the next cycle requires emptying your cup of that previous experience. That happens during that process that is called mindfulness. The lesson that we learn is not a conceptual lesson. Rather we are taught what will be required in order to have each new experience be more profound than the last. That teaching is not intellectual: it is experiential and natural. I will close this chapter with the following thought, which I take from Joe Hyams' book, *Zen in the Martial Arts*:

> The master poured his visitor's cup full and then kept on pouring.
>
> The professor watched the cup overflowing until he could no longer restrain himself. 'The cup is overfull, no more will go in.'
>
> 'Like this cup,' the master said, 'you are full of your own opinions and speculations. How can I show you Zen unless you first empty your cup?' [16]

116

CHAPTER SIX

WORK WITH, DON'T ELIMINATE
RESISTANCE

No great improvements in the lot of mankind are possible
until a great change takes place in the fundamental
constitution of their modes of thought.

John Stuart Mill

How do you think about someone or something that you believe has wronged you? Maybe it was a parent or bully. Maybe it was a hurricane or accident. Wouldn't it be great if that person or event had never been part of your life?

I know a man by the name of Ron Heagy. Ron is a well-known speaker who helps people with this very question. Ron is a quadriplegic who, as a teenager, had an accident while swimming that left him paralyzed from the neck down. Ron says in his presentations, that he does not regret what happened to him. He says that the amazing people he has met, the places that he has been, and the experiences he has had would never have happened if that accident hadn't occurred.

Ron lives a very active and inspired life with his beautiful wife, Kelli and their children. It is clear from his presentations that

Ron does not live in the world of regrets and "if only's." That is because he doesn't try to eliminate resistance but rather he is a master at working with it. That fundamental way of thinking keeps Ron in flow, always being moved by what inspires him while at the same time appreciating the ever-changing journey.

Consider that it isn't the people or events that you encounter in your life that cause you to fail but rather your resistance to them. Working with resistance doesn't mean that you don't get upset and experience pain and it doesn't mean that life is a bed of roses. It means that you stay connected to whatever breathes life into you and you don't lose that connection during the sometimes challenging and chaotic process of the co-creation of your life's journey.

No resistance, no experience

Instead of thinking of your intention or best idea in terms of its desired outcome, you can think of your intention in terms of its higher purpose, which is creative experience. Creative experience is an active and inspiring cycle where you work with resistance using influence, not control.

What does that mean? It means that you let go of the specific concepts that you have created to define a particular cycle. So, for example, you let go of your inspiring idea as being important and of your performance in action as being important. And you also let go of your brilliant conclusions or learning or achievements or failures as important.

Instead, you consider it important that the inspired idea you hold is the influencing factor throughout your experience. You consider it important that you do not default to another idea designed to control external things and people in order to keep your experience within your comfort zone.

Working with resistance is not about focusing on resistance. That will simply start a new cycle founded on a useless idea. Working with resistance is more effectively accomplished by accepting it. Be willing to proceed with your best ideas accepting resistance not as something to be eliminated but rather as something to be appreciated as part of the creative process. That which you are resisting will influence and be influenced by you because in any interaction of energy fields both you and what you are integrating with are impacted.

Challenge yourself

An inspired idea is by its nature a call to discover the expansive possibilities of your capacity for experience. It is a natural function of desire to move out of your comfort zone and into your discovery zone. Inspired ideas are the first phase of creative experience.

You might feel that those new ideas are very challenging. It can feel like what is being challenged is your own security. Rather than an opportunity for discovery, you might see your inspired idea as a challenge to what you already have. In other words, you may understand transition into action as risky. And it is: you are risking what you have, even though what you have may or may not be particularly exciting to you.

How can you allow that transition in the face of the possibility of loss? If you understand that what you have is the capacity for experience, then you have nothing to lose. That is because new experience, whether good or bad, will simply add to that capacity. If you understand that what you have are material things, then you stand to lose everything because in the experiential cycle, those things don't exist in any permanent form. They must be recreated over and over. Thus, you have actually created the illusion that they exist in some permanent form by

119

endlessly re-creating them. If, however, the recreation of those "things" is for the purpose of security rather than discovery, then you might find yourself in the Grail King's Waste Land of contracting rather than expanding experience.

Recreating something over and over is a worthwhile effort if in recreating it you are discovering new and expanding experience each time. For example, in a rewarding relationship with a significant other, the nature of the time spent together is discovery-oriented. You recreate that time together over and over because it is always new and fresh. The relationship is experience expanding because both people are authentic and both support optimal influence.

In an unrewarding relationship, the nature of being together is security-oriented. The unrewarding relationship is recreated over and over as the result of an illusion: in this case, the preservation of an imagined experience that holds on to a concept of the other person rather than the experience with the other person. In an unrewarding relationship, what you think you will lose if you let it go is something you never had in the first place.

Holding on to a concept does not preserve a good experience; in fact, it will very likely deaden it. Experience is heightened by personal expansion through ongoing natural cycles founded on an inspired and often challenging idea. When you are searching for security, you won't look in the place where inspired ideas are found. You will look instead in concepts designed to control and fix things in place.

William Blake's short poem, "Eternity," serves to illustrate the nature of personal expansion:

> He who binds to himself a joy
> Does the winged life destroy.
> But he who kisses the joy as it flies
> Lives in eternity's sun rise. [17]

It can be challenging to let go of joyful people and experiences. Fear can surface out of concern that they will not return or that life will never be as good again. Blake warns us about resisting the very nature that creates that joy in the first place. He urges us to trust our nature, not our concepts.

Challenge can be thought of as part of the experiential process. No challenge - no experience and no personal expansion. You might think of what Blake says in line 1 about "binding to himself a joy," as being a good goal – hold on to what is good. Remember, however, that as good as something might seem at first, it is only through change that joy occurs in the first place. Don't allow an experience of joy to turn into a concept that restricts you.

In your life, you sometimes feel the need to possess what you take to be valuable. Thus, when you are laid off from a job that you enjoyed, you can become despondent thinking of the loss as the loss of joy itself. How often do you later find that the change actually brought you to a new life level you hadn't experienced in years? Why? Maybe because you had so identified your idea of the job as the joy itself, that you had smothered change and therefore the opportunity to experience new things. It is like thinking that the value of a beautiful sunset exists in the sun rather than in your capacity for experience.

In Blake's poem "Eternity," "he who kisses the joy as it flies" is a person who appreciates the good things in life and lets go easily, not because these good things are unimportant but because of a deeper understanding of change. As a result, he experiences life as "living in eternity's sun rise." With that approach, each new day has some level of challenge and with that challenge and change comes the opportunity for deeper experience.

Challenge yourself by being willing to allow and engage in inspiring ideas. You are much more than you think if you understand your true nature as an infinite capacity for energetic experience. Some of what you let go will come back and some will make way for new and rewarding experience.

Manage to let go of yourself

How do you let go of yourself? When you started this book, I suggested you discover who you are because who you are determines what you do. Now I am suggesting that you let go of yourself. How can this apparently contradictory advice be helpful?

There are many levels of who you are. There are those immediate daily responses that result in self-talk that might sound like, "I am a loser" or "I am so cool." Then there are the longer term and higher-level ideas like, "I am a man" or "I am a woman."

The key is that in every case, who you are starts off as ideas or concepts, which begin to manifest your current energy. And as such, they will naturally lead to action and learning. In order to be fresh and inspired in your experience, you will want to let go of all previous conclusions so that each experience can integrate into your collective awareness. All experiences include all of the ideas associated with those experiences. Since who you are is an idea that began a previous cycle, you will want to let it go, which means letting go of yourself.

If that idea of who you are was one that connected with your core energy, then it will probably show up again with the birth of your new and inspired idea. Your intention here is not to banish every idea you have ever had. It is to send it into collective awareness and see if it comes up again as part of an inspired you.

Some people are inspired by the idea of being a doctor. They were inspired in that way when they were 22 and they are still inspired in the same way at 62. The point is to continually check in with collective awareness to find out who you are today. If that is the same as yesterday, then that is great. If it is not the same, then you will want to know that.

Manage to let go of yourself so that you can discover whether your core energy is still creating that same inspired idea. If so, then go for it. If not, then allow your core energy to reveal a new inspired you.

Summary

Resistance is all in your head. And it is all about controlling what is external. "I want to have a lot of money" or "I want to have a great relationship" are often ideas that resonate with people. As with a stream, there are often things that seem to get in the way of having the money or the great relationship. The path sometimes seems strewn with the rocks and boulders I describe in the introduction to Part Two.

The rocks and boulders will never keep you from the money and relationships you want. Your resistance to their being there will, however. Why? Because when you go into resistance, you substitute a new primary idea for your natural inspirational gravity and that new idea will be what you don't want, i.e. the boulders. Since you are a resonant being, the fact that you *don't* want a boulder has the same effect as the exercise you did in Chapter One when I said, *don't* look at anything red. All you will see is boulders and those ideas will become the primary ideas for your Natural Experiential Cycles. The result? No progress in money or relationships and more boulders to fight. Three things can help.

Recognize that resistance is most likely to show up at the three points: between ideas and action, action and learning, or learning and a new idea. Get to know what it feels like for you when you go into resistance and be aware of the fear that is usually underneath the logical reasons you give yourself.

Experience will change you. That is the point. You are energy continually taking on new forms and in those new forms lies the experience you want. Be willing to be changed. Don't get stuck in or on a cycle. Each cycle is an experience and each new cycle provides the opportunity for a new experience. That is the nature of your expanding capacity for experience.

Finally, you do live in the real world. It is useful to know that boulders and barriers are out there. So work with those boulders and the resistance that you feel when they seem to be in the way rather than trying to eliminate them. When you work with resistance, you will both influence and be influenced by that creative integration of energy. If there were no resistance and no challenge, there would also be no experience. Allow yourself to move into the discovery zone and be challenged. Just don't forget your primary inspired idea or *inspirational gravity* in the midst of a challenge. Also, know who you are and then, when the time is right, be willing to let go of yourself so that a new knowing and a new you can occur after each cycle is complete.

PART THREE

STAYING GROUNDED EVERY DAY

I always wanted to be somebody. I should have been more specific.

Lily Tomlin

There is a split second in time when you make a choice that determines whether you will make the quantum leap to inspired experience or not. Whether the choice is in the arena of making more money, starting a new business, taking a dream trip or committing to any of the incredible things that you imagine - it is simply the choice of what idea to believe in.

That decision point occurs in an actual time and place in the real world and it happens when you are feeling resistance to what is natural. In that instant, you will either go unconscious and default to an old idea that will result in an old action or you will choose to stay conscious and hold on to your new inspired idea and find a way to move forward toward your natural energetic destination. It is choice, not luck, skill or talent that makes the difference.

How long does it take you to change from one idea to another in your mind? Whatever the duration, that is how long it takes to resist your own success. Consider that your essence is energy. Energy wants to move naturally. Think, for example, of electricity or energy in the air. In a thunderstorm, energy wants to go to "ground." That lightening bolt that you see is energy on the move. Notice that it doesn't move in a straight line. Just as the journeys of inspired lives are jagged or crooked, so too, is the bolt's path to its destination. The path of success is usually not a conceptual straight line. It is an experiential discovery.

A Natural Experiential Cycle is like a lightening bolt. It is your energy naturally grounding you by going from an idea to action and then to learning. Staying grounded every day is allowing that Natural Cycle to occur without resisting the idea that the path is filled with so called obstacles. It is during the interplay between you and those obstacles that creation happens.

Any time you choose to default to an idea that is not connected to your creative energy, you are also choosing to become ungrounded. You are disconnecting from the origin of value, which is creative energy, and its experiential path through resistance and you are attempting to connect to an external source or concept for value. Your energy does not come from the concept of external things and that disconnect will leave you ungrounded and unfulfilled. When you feel resistance, stay conscious no matter how uncomfortable the path feels: in other words, remember the idea that inspired you and allow that inspirational gravity to naturally create optimal influence.

CHAPTER SEVEN

HAVE A ROUTINE TO
CONNECT WITH INSPIRATION

*What concerns me is not the way things are, but rather the
way people think things are.*

Epictetus

Life happens daily. New ideas, new actions, and new learning
happen moment to moment. Resisting what is happening takes
you out of the present moment. When you are *working with*
resistance you stay in the present. This current moment is the only
time and place where optimal influence can create something
fulfilling. It can be useful to have a way to bring yourself back into
the present each day or whenever you feel challenged by
resistance. To do so will help keep your day flowing towards what
you really want in your life.

Much of what has been presented in this book so far are ideas
and new ways to think about things. The natural cycle is then for
you to begin to allow these ideas to transition into action. So, it
can be useful to have some specific things to do that will begin to
manifest these ideas. It could be that if you wait until tomorrow or
next week to begin doing something tangible about any resonant

ideas in this book, then you are experiencing resistance. If so, don't judge yourself for it but do be aware of it. Remember, the first key to better flow in your life is recognizing resistance when it occurs.

So, I have provided a few suggestions for things to do in order to allow these ideas to move into action. You can't do them wrong or right and you will want to change or adapt them for what works best for you. It is the intention of these processes that is important not the method.

Clear a path for experience

It isn't enough to have a new plan or concept for how you are going to hold on to your best ideas. As you can see from the Natural Experiential Cycle model, you must allow that idea to transition into action. The action that I suggest will happen on a daily basis. You will want to be conscious every day in order to best manage the resistance that can send you back to an old idea and stuck in an unproductive cycle.

So I suggest that you create a routine for your day that will help you do that. Also, I suggest that you review your routine every now and then in order to make adjustments that will keep it useful. To help you in developing such a plan, I am providing you with some of the things I do to help myself. You can use them as is or you can make adjustments to fit your lifestyle and preferences.

Morning

1. Mindfulness Cues

The first thing I do is to say what I call a mindfulness cue or "mind-cue" for short. The intention of the mind-cue is to make conscious the letting go of yesterday's experiences (or any cycle of experience that is ending) and be fully present today. It is simple and not a religious event although it can look a little like a prayer or affirmation. The structure of a mind cue has four parts.

First, I make myself conscious of the creative and, therefore, moldable nature of all things. This is meant to remind me that both my circumstances and myself are in continual, purposeful change and if things don't seem to be changing it is because I am recreating the same thing over and over again.

Second, I express gratitude for the phase of the cycle that is completing and ask for what I want next. This helps me stay conscious of where I am in the natural cycle and what naturally follows.

Third, I remind myself that any resistance I experience is based on fear, which can disconnect me from my passion. This clears the way so that I can be fully present in moving through the phases of the Cycle.

Finally, I release myself to move forward in the cycle without being tied to expectations and remind myself that the day (or next event) will evolve in a co-creative way. This is meant to acknowledge the idea that neither side must disconnect from their own inspirational gravity.

One variation of my morning mind-cue is as follows.

Letting go of learning to allow inspired ideas:
I am aware just now of the creative energy that surrounds, fills, and is me and ask to be conscious of its ongoing guidance and support in this new day. I am grateful for the learning that I have gained through [*"yesterday's experience"*] and just now, I let that learning go into collective awareness. I release any resistance that I might have at this time and so that I am moved by my passion. I look forward to [*this day*] with fresh eyes and fresh inspiration fully

connected with all that is and ask for the highest good for all concerned.

This mind-cue is one that I often say in the morning. Those same four elements can be useful, however, anytime I get stuck in some kind of judgment or conclusions about someone or something. You can use my mind-cue or make one up for yourself by just including those four elements.

2. Meditation/relaxation

The intention of doing this in the morning is to move from the idea of my mind-cue into an action of mindfulness by clearing my mind of any attachment to yesterday's cycles. In other words, I want completion and I want to let go of any conclusions or judgments that might be persisting. That way, when I choose my best ideas for the day, they will come from collective awareness and not from some holdover of yesterday's successes or failures. You can do a simple relaxation exercise or meditation to help let go.

Eastern philosophies sometimes use a mental exercise called mindfulness meditation. You have already seen the word "mindfulness" in my discussion of the Natural Experiential Cycle model. As I stated earlier, it is the practice of being present in a way that does not attach to any particular ideas or thoughts that might arise in the mind. Relaxing, closing your eyes, and then being aware of all of the thoughts that come into your mind is a way to experience it. You can think of each thought as being like a cloud floating by. You are aware of it and when it passes, you simply allow your attention to move to the next cloud and so on.

Another way of practicing or experiencing mindfulness is to be aware of your breathing. As each breath is completed, you simply allow your attention to move to the next breath without attaching emotionally or conceptually to the previous breath.

During this practice, you are completely aware. Ideas come to you naturally. And you let each idea go by allowing your attention to move on.

In my meditation, maintaining breath-awareness is often what I do. It tends to bring me present and it helps me to let go of any achievements, failures, conclusions, judgments, and so forth that might have occurred yesterday. I let them go in the same way I let go of the awareness of each thought in my meditation. I don't resist any thought. To do so would be like the water resisting a rock or boulder that it encountered on its trip down the hill. My intention in doing this exercise is to allow my collective awareness to begin providing ideas for my new day by clearing a path for them to come when they are ready.

3. Yoga

Next, I sometimes do a set of simple yoga exercises. I really do this for the same reason that I do the mindfulness meditation. I have brought myself mentally present and now I want to clear my body of any "physical memories" of yesterday and be physically present as well.

You can do any kind of simple exercise or even put on some music you like and move around the room to the feel of the music in order to get the same result. This doesn't require a hard workout: in fact, a hard workout might be counter-productive because it usually has a specific intention or outcome behind it like losing weight or improving body tone. Since you are trying to clear your mind and body of all old ideas, intentions, conclusions, and so on, a hard workout might not be helpful. You can save the intentional physical exercise for after you have tapped into your collective awareness.

4. Journal - Review & choose daily idea

The third thing I do is to spend a few minutes journaling. I have a spiral school-type notebook and my journaling intention is to come up with my best ideas. I allow myself to write about whatever comes to mind knowing that what I get down will lead to one or more ideas that will inspire me for the day. My journaling is not just free thought although it is free flowing. My intention is to see where my energy is and by allowing my writing to be free flowing, two things can happen. First, leftover energy from the previous day has a way to reach completion and second, I can connect to the energy that is inspiring me today. Out of today's energy can come the central idea that will guide much of today's activities. After I complete my journaling, I usually tear up what I have written and throw it away so that it doesn't become a fixed concept or judgment that could hold me back.

5. "Next actions" list

Once I have found my exciting and motivating idea for the day, I then create a "next actions" list being sure my best idea is allowed to transition into some kind of action that day.

Many of the things I do during my day might not be related to my best idea. I might need to check in with my daughters, make a bank deposit, call a potential client and so forth. My intention isn't necessarily to spend the whole day around my inspiring idea or big dream. It is to be consciously aware of what my best ideas are and to allow those ideas to naturally influence others and me. It is also to move those ideas to some kind of completion, no matter how small or seemingly insignificant. That experiential completion and letting go is essential if I am to expand my collective awareness in a way that keeps my experience founded on my most inspiring ideas. In other words, my intention is to have a day that grows out of energy and inspiration rather than just a job to do.

I want my completions to continue around my best idea so that I can integrate it into collective awareness. That integration will then reveal another new idea that I could not have had without having gone through that sometimes small but very significant cycle.

I want to add one additional thought about your best idea and next actions. As a child, you might have experienced times when your parents, teachers, or other authority figures disregarded or even discouraged you when you expressed excitement about your dreams or what you wanted. You might have concluded that you couldn't have the things that excited you. While belief about whether you can have what you want is important, there is the possibility that something deeper and more destructive happened when the adults in your life discouraged you. You might have come to believe that *words themselves* weren't important. In other words, those people didn't just bring into question whether you could have what you want; they also took away the mechanism for getting what you want.

Knowing what you know now about the Natural Experiential Cycle, you should realize just how important words are. They are the beginning of the creative cycle of manifestation. Since words are creative, it is very important that you put into words what your intention is for your day, especially with regard to what inspires you. Clarifying your dream with words that specify today's next action is the beginning of the manifestation of that dream. There are times when we can have fun and even be somewhat irreverent with our words and there are times when we need to acknowledge and use their power carefully. Believe that your inspired ideas and the words you use to express them on your next actions list (and in your conversations) are critically important!

6. Transition into action

Once my next actions list is complete for the day, I continue to transition into action. Writing the list is part of the flow of transition from idea to action. Doing what I have indicated on the list is the continuation of that transition into action. It is important to be aware of how you write your list in order to best support transition. For best results, check your list for actual next actions.

For example, writing on your list "plan a trip to Paris" is not a next action. It is too general and will require more thought before actual activity can occur. A good next action might be "visit travel agency to get brochures on Paris." That is a specific activity that can be completed today. Writing, "plan a trip to Paris" is not a next action and might even suggest some resistance about taking action if it shows up on your "next actions list." Instead, put it on your projects list and only put actual things you can do currently on your next actions list. You might find that when you have things on your "to do" or "next actions" list that are general and don't really offer a specific next action, you are actually experiencing some level of resistance and are avoiding in some way. It is almost like pretending you want to do something but avoiding action by keeping the wording conceptual rather than active.

As your day progresses, be aware of what you are doing and thinking, and check for delay or avoidance. It might suggest resistance. Below is a short mind-cue that I sometimes use when I am feeling resistance to taking action on one of my best ideas.

Transition from idea to action:

I am aware just now of the creative energy that surrounds, fills, and is me and ask to be conscious of its ongoing guidance and support in this moment. I know that creative energy is always becoming and that my current idea which starts as very subtle energy will naturally move into action. I release any resistance I might feel as this idea begins to manifest and allow myself to influence and be influenced by this natural co-creative process. I am taking action with a consious awareness that is fully connected to my inspirational gravity and ask for the highest good for all concerned.

7. Manage resistance

The next thing I do is more of an all-day process. Resistance can show up at any time and is part of every day. If there isn't any, then I am probably not challenging myself. My intention here is simply to be conscious of the occurrence of resistance and to recognize and work with it as effectively as possible when I experience it.

As I say in Chapter 6, the way I deal with resistance is to not resist it. In other words, I allow resistance and don't see it as something to be eliminated. Moreover, I allow not only the resistance, but also the fear that usually lies beneath it. Often, just allowing my own resistance will lead to constructive action in a way that simply attempts to influence things rather than control them.

In a way, once you assume that you will experience pain (and that you don't need to hold onto it), you remove its power over you and the resistance disappears. At the same time, you will usually not want to create situations where the pain or challenge will be excessive. Your intention is not to inflict pain on yourself

135

or anyone else. Your goal is to stay connected to that which moves you, much like water in a stream that responds to gravity and flows toward the ocean. You simply allow the rocks and boulders that are part of the journey to influence the nature of that journey.

Resistance could show up at any time in any of the three phases of the cycle (transition, completion, and letting go). For example, if your idea is to write a book and you write down a next action for the day as "write a book," you might run into some resistance to such a large and general task. So, rather than abandoning the idea, you can simply choose a next action that transitions the idea into less challenging action. You might simply start by creating a book title. In this way, your response to resistance was to allow it to influence what you chose for your next action. But it did not cause you to abandon your inspiring idea.

If you don't like any of the titles you have created and the day is turning into night, you can just choose the best one you have and call your action complete. Then, let go of any judgments about whether the title is good or bad and allow the experience to move into your collective awareness. You can continue to improve it as the days go by. The key is to stay in flow during the day by working with any resistance that occurs.

Evening

8. Completions list

At the end of the day, I often write down my completions for the day. I don't necessarily write down everything I have completed, but I might write down any completions related to my best ideas. Writing them down is a physical act that helps me declare them complete experientially. One to five completions is generally what I do.

There are two aspects to this completion process. One is conceptual and the other experiential. I actually force them to work together. The way I do that is to create a concept that fits my experience. So, for example, if I started the day with the concept of finding a title for my new book and at the end of the day I don't have one that I am satisfied with, I simply change my concept to something like, come up with three ideas for book titles. So, the fact that I have three titles is an accomplishment even though it didn't match the concept of a great book title by evening. I make the concept fit with whatever I came up with. That not only allows conceptual completion, but it also supports experiential completion. Experientially, it is the end of the day and I am tired and energetically done. Leaving the concept in an incomplete state can leave me experientially incomplete.

It would be like running a race and only completing half of it because of a pulled muscle. The race is over and holding on to a logical concept of the finish line as the end is resisting my own experience. My completions list is true, meaning it coincides with my experience.

That doesn't mean that I am lazy and reduced to blind luck in terms of my accomplishments. The Natural Experiential Cycle is a natural process and it will tend to have me living in a very productive way. If I work with resistance well during the day, there is a good chance I might even have that great book title when I am done. When you are in sync with the Natural Experiential Cycle, you are also in sync with your own optimum energy levels. It is that creative energy that gets things done, not harsh self-judgment. Making experiential and conceptual cycles coincide is part of the process of letting go. It is insisting that you see things as they are rather than what you wish they were.

Wishing that things were different can bring up judgment about unrealized expectations and keep you attached to old cycles.

9. Disconnect – meditate/exercise

Having acknowledged various completions, I make a conscious effort to let my subconscious know that completion has occurred. I might do a simple meditation or exercise to help work with any resistance to completion and learning. Below is a mind-cue that I sometimes use to help me maximize my natural learning through completion.

> Completion of action for learning:
> I am aware just now of the creative energy that surrounds, fills, and is me and ask to be conscious of its ongoing guidance and support. I know that [*"the activities of this day"*] are now complete and open up to the learning for me. I allow true completion both conceptually and experientially to occur and release any resistance that I might feel as completion reveals new learning for the highest good of all concerned.

The true learning that occurs is informational rather than emotional. If it is emotional then it is likely that true completion has not yet occurred. If this is the case, don't judge yourself. Simply take additional steps to support completion.

After using the mind-cues a number of times (transition, completion and letting go), you will probably find that you will simply become aware that you are in one of the three points of resistance and the essence of the mind-cue will come to you without actually saying it. Along with that essence will come the sense of being present that accompanies mindfulness and the experience of flow in your life.

138

10. Celebrate

Finally, on my list is to celebrate. Celebration is not necessarily throwing a party. In fact, it usually isn't unless I have completed something very significant that, like a rite of passage, requires a little more emphasis on gratitude and letting go. For me on a typical night, my celebration occurs at dinnertime. Whether my dinner consists of a hamburger, spaghetti, or steak, it is often a time when I consciously mark an end to the day and note something to celebrate, whether pleasurable or painful. *The American Heritage Dictionary of the English Language* defines the word celebrate as follows: "to observe (a day or event) with ceremonies of respect or festivity." Whether respectful or festive, my intention is to consciously begin the process of integrating the day's experience into collective awareness.

You can do something like what I do or you could do something different. You could, for example, journal before you go to bed or review the day with a spouse or friend. It is also a good idea to help children get into that same habit of celebration by talking with them at dinner or before bed with that same intention of bringing the day to experiential (and conceptual) completion. Regardless of how you choose to end the day remember, it is a time meant to acknowledge learning and begin to let it go, i.e. allow it to become information rather than emotion. It is not an exercise in judging and holding on to something.

I don't always follow this daily process and do everything that I have listed above. Many days I resist doing it (and consciously allow that resistance) and many days I get up energized and move quickly into action. It seems that sleep can have its own impact on where I am in a cycle when I wake up.

I don't resist whatever is happening in the morning. Many mornings and during the day I find the process I described above is very helpful in getting off to an energized start and staying in flow. You might find the same.

Wait for inspiration

Inspiration is more like a discovery than an achievement. Since you are energy, you don't start the day wondering if you will be able to create something. Creativity isn't a question; it simply is. If there is a question, it is whether you will recognize inspirational ideas (whether large or small) when they appear.

If you become impatient for an idea that inspires you, you are in resistance to that natural process. In other words, you have created some kind of conceptual belief about how that process should occur. Your experiential cycle may or may not match that original conceptual cycle. It has been said that Einstein got some of his best ideas in the shower. He was tuned into his experience rather than conceptual expectations.

In fact, the idea that some great inspiration will occur on any particular day is also a concept. The idea that comes up for you today might be to relax. That can certainly be understood as inspirational because sometimes just relaxing will breath new life into you. Energy knows what to do. It knows when it is at a high point and it knows when it is renewing itself. Your job is to stay connected to it so that you can be naturally directed by it.

You will want to be patient throughout every Natural Experiential Cycle so that you are not resisting what is natural. To be patient does not mean that you are not committed, active and completing things. It just means that you are committed to your energetic core and that your logical concepts are the servant and not the master of that creative energy.

Ground what inspires you

Grounding the life that inspires you happens when you are willing to work with the resistance that gives your experience its creative nature. Experience is not creative and personally expansive unless it is grounded in the three points of resistance. It is during the processes of transition, completion, and letting go that resistance creates you in the same way that boulders and rocks create the path of a stream. Allowing an inspired idea to move into action and then learning means that you pass through those thresholds of resistance in creative ways.

The challenge you feel when you allow an inspired idea to transition into action changes you in ways you cannot put into words and certainly in ways you cannot predict. Taking action brings energy into focus and you can literally feel it in the real world. The shift in energy you feel when you allow action to move to completion and learning also changes you in unexpected ways. Win or lose, succeed or fail, something unique happens in your energetic awareness when an experience is complete. And finally, when learning is let go, a renewal in energy takes place that reconnects you with your creative and energetic essence.

Ground what inspires you through the transition of ideas, completion of activity, and letting go of learning. You will stay grounded to the extent that you experience these things as an ongoing flow like a river, rather than a state that you can reach. Being fixed in any way does not ground you. It is simply a sign that you are resisting the idea of the rocks and boulders in your stream instead of allowing the creative play of optimal influence as you are continuously pulled by your inspirational gravity.

The idea that you will be happy and grounded once you achieve a certain state misses the core nature of you as energy. Energy wants to be in a state of flux. That sounds like a paradox since "state" suggests a fixed idea and "flux" suggests a changing one. The paradox comes from an effort to reduce who you are to a concept. You are an idea. And you are also action and learning (knowledge). The integration or totality of who and what you are can only be experienced. If your goal is controlling your experience in order to avoid pain, you become stuck. While being stuck is also an experience, it's often very boring and feels like personal contraction instead of personal expansion.

CHAPTER EIGHT

CELEBRATE TO INTEGRATE

*One can never change the past, only the hold
it has on you.*

Merle Shain

You have the amazing gift of renewal. You are not attached to your history much as it might seem that way sometimes. The Natural Experiential Cycle will take care of your history if you allow it. You are free to do and be what you want and you don't have to learn how to bring about that change. Since renewal is a natural gift, you have only to work with your resistance and it will happen naturally.

That phase in the Cycle where completion and learning occur often brings up powerful moments of fear and self-doubt. There is no need to try to eliminate those feelings. To attempt to do so is to try to eliminate resistance. One way to help you work with resistance is to go conscious of the end that has occurred. Having a celebration can serve that purpose. We do it at weddings, funerals, baby showers and all kinds of other passages of change.

Making a big deal about the end of something is intended to clearly tell the sub-conscious mind to stop working on that old experience. You will want to take the energy out of definitions and structures created in the past and allow that energy to go back into undefined collective awareness. From there the renewal of energy can occur with the birth of your new idea and the definitions and structures that will naturally evolve.

Gratitude, not self-importance

People often don't celebrate enough, and when they do, it's often not for the most beneficial purpose. Celebrating your own achievement or greatness is not as useful as celebrating experience itself. You are thankful for the opportunity to engage in these Natural Experiential Cycles and you celebrate that opportunity with gratitude rather than judgments about self-importance. A celebration of acknowledgement and gratitude is directed toward the expanding nature of your capacity for awareness. Acknowledgement and gratitude tend to support expansion.

Celebrating, as a rite of passage and way to let go, can be very helpful in terms of the effect it has on completing a cycle and opening you up to new and exciting ideas. It allows your experience to be very fulfilling on an ongoing basis because it does not let you become attached to specific emotionally charged events that you have conceptualized.

When you attach to specific events, your life feels more like a yo-yo with your experience going up and down and the feeling that you are at the mercy of whatever happens today. This doesn't mean that you don't celebrate a specific event like a wedding or birthday or business success. It simply means that you don't attach experience to any external event or person.

Remember: it isn't the sunset that has value. It is your ability to experience it in a meaningful way. And so in the same way that you might say, "what a beautiful sunset," you might also say, "I am so excited about opening my new business." You will engage fully in the celebration and you will remain grateful for simply having a nature that creates that experience and awareness. You will recognize that your capacity to experience at all is a gift not an achievement.

Celebrate often and completely engage in the celebration. It will help you to manifest completion and let go so that the experience can integrate into your collective awareness. At the same time, express gratitude in some way for the fact that you can experience anything at all. That gratitude will help keep you from moving into resistance and getting stuck.

Be conscious of outcome

Know that results indicate intention. What does that mean? It means that if you want to know what you want at your deepest levels, then take a look at what you have. If what you have doesn't seem to be what you want, then you probably have a subconscious program running that is based on fear. And that program is intercepting your inspiring ideas and shooting them down because of what it tells you might go wrong. It is putting you into a conditional mindset. A conditional mindset says to you that you can't have what you want until certain conditions have been met. And those conditions are that you won't experience pain or loss. Those conditions are all about resistance to the boulders and rocks that you think shouldn't be there.

As a result of this conditional thinking, your deepest want is for security, not for what inspiration might bring you. The outcome is that you must do what you don't want to do, forever. Why forever? Because discovery by its nature includes some kind of discomfort or pain. As long as you resist the pain and discomfort that can accompany discovery, you are like a river that has come to a stop because it resents whatever seems to be in its way.

The purpose of knowing that *results indicate intention* is so that you can find out what is really motivating and directing you. Your circumstances are not the result of bad luck or what someone else has done to you. As a creative being, you are creating everything in your life. You have no choice about being creative.

So, whatever you have, you have created. If you have created out of what you fear, then you probably don't have what you are inspired to have. And you probably aren't having much fun. If you are creating out of love – that is what you love to do and what you love to be - then you probably have what you are inspired to have. And you are probably having fun. As a creative being, your outcome will indicate your intention.

Pain happens in this life. Everything around you has an energetic effect and influences you. You can choose to resist pain and in that resistance you can shift to a fear consciousness. That shift will have you resonating with painful circumstances that then create more of those painful outcomes. You create that outcome because of setting an intention that resonates with fear.

You need to know what you are doing in order to stop doing it. Blaming your circumstances on someone or something else denies your creative nature. It suggests that someone else can make you focus on a particular idea. Influence is different than control. Your creative nature can't be controlled because it has it's own built-in control mechanism. You can influence what is happening in your life even in the face of traumatic events. The idea that you can't suggests that you can't go over, under, or around rocks and boulders in your stream. You can. You can allow events to influence you without giving up control of what ideas you choose to hold (believe).

The way to discover your controlling unconscious ideas is to be conscious of outcome. Once you know that your deeper intention is fear-based, then you can work with resistance and choose more inspired ideas in order to create a new outcome. The cause and effect nature of experiential cycles guarantees your creative independence.

If you accept that cause and effect nature of the cycle, then you can see how the ideas you hold as beliefs will manifest in every aspect of your life. For example, you might say to yourself, "Because of my financial circumstances, my boss controls my life. I have to work late and do whatever s/he tells me to do." In that example, you are disconnecting from your power and inspiration by stating a creative idea that will have you doing whatever your boss needs done. The idea will manifest as long as you hold it as a belief or initial idea in a cycle. Creative energy controls your life and that means that you can influence any situation simply by allowing your best idea to begin to manifest in your current situation.

You might ask yourself, "why am I in this situation?" Since you are a creative being, there are no accidents. Is it your fault or is it your boss's fault. Who cares? For the creative being, the question is not why this happened or whose fault it is. Why it happened is because people are creative beings and fault lies in the nature of optimal influence where both exert influence. A better question can be "how did this happen?" How are you creating your current income? What ideas are you holding on to that are revealed by the results that you are getting? How can you create a different outcome? How can you influence your current situation with a new idea? Once you know how you are creating the situations in which you find yourself, you can choose to do something different by choosing more empowering ideas. The question, "why" indicates resistance. You know why because of the cause and effect nature of experience. The question is how can you create a different outcome and the answer is by choosing *and believing* a different idea.

147

Gather information, not judgments

During the third phase of the Natural Experiential Cycle, a choice is made as to whether the outcome will become information or judgments. Judgments will keep recreating an experience by providing the trigger ideas for new cycles. Judgments suggest resistance to letting go. Information will allow new experience by integrating all aspects of the cycle completed into collective awareness. Information becomes known and is then let go for possible future use. Judgments are assigned the label of truth and are then held on to.

In *The Hero with a Thousand Faces*, Joseph Campbell quotes from the Bhagavad Gita:

"Even as a person casts off worn-out clothes and puts on others that are new, so the embodied Self casts off worn-out bodies and enters into others that are new. . . Eternal, all-pervading, unchanging, immovable, the Self is the same for ever."

Man in the world of action loses his centering in the principle of eternity if he is anxious for the outcome of his deeds, but resting them and their fruits on the knees of the Living God he is released by them, as by a sacrifice, from the bondages of the sea of death. "Do without attachment the work you have to do. . . Surrendering all action to Me, with mind intent on the Self, freeing yourself from longing and selfishness, fight – unperturbed by grief." [18]

As I understand it, the worn-out clothes to which the Bhagavad Gita refers are judgments and conclusions about one's self and one's actions. Beliefs can limit us. As I said earlier, beliefs aren't true but they are creative. They create repetitive experiences. Sometimes beliefs are useful and sometimes they are not.

When energy begins to create defined patterns or manifest, it also begins to appear: first in the mind as an idea and then in a

148

specific time and place as action. Judgments tend to freeze the spirit in time and space by attaching themselves to an idea or belief that might be conditionally true, but not energetically true. This attachment shuts us off from that Self that is not tied to a particular idea or a particular place in time and space but rather, is the creator of those ideas.

Judgments (and beliefs) bind you to the conceptual conclusions of a past experience. Information moves that learning into collective awareness where it is no longer tied to anything. Judgments contain old energy while information is energy-free once integrated into collective awareness. From that place it can expand your capacity for experience by contributing to discovery.

CHAPTER NINE

LET GO TO BE POWERFULLY PRESENT

*Technical knowledge is not enough. One must transcend
techniques so that the art becomes an artless art, growing
out of the unconscious.*

Daisetsu Suzuki

The gift of the birth of new ideas and a new you requires a
return to formlessness or what I call collective awareness. You will
not experience the joy and thrill of renewal through some logical
effort to fix things. The process of fixing things is the gift of the
Natural Experiential Cycle. Renewal is our nature not something
we must achieve. Part of that natural process requires that we let it
happen rather than trying to make it happen. While a doctor can
set a broken bone s/he cannot make the two pieces of bone grow
back together again. The goal of the doctor is to help create the
best possible environment where that natural process can occur. It
is also the most useful goal of parents, business managers, and all
leaders to create such an environment. Trying to make things
happen for yourself or others actually suggests resistance to the
Natural Experiential Cycle. That effort tends to usurp the
uniqueness of each individual's inspiration and it aims for control

rather than co-creation and discovery. So it is with you and your own self-leadership.

Making your days the adventure they are designed to be requires that you let go in order to return to that state of mindfulness described by Gunaratan in Chapter Four as a, "fleeting instant of pure awareness just before you conceptualize the thing . . ." In other words, you let go of all of your cares and concerns and allow yourself to return to formlessness so that inspiration can create new form through the experience of a Natural Experiential Cycle.

Such an experience is sometimes referred to as being in "flow" in sports. It is typically a very rewarding and fulfilling experience. In the book, *Flow in Sports, The keys to optimal experiences and performances*, flow is defined as follows: "First of all, it is a state of consciousness where one becomes totally absorbed in what one is doing, to the exclusion of all other thoughts and emotions." [19] The requirement of letting go is central to fulfillment and personal expansion.

Let go to allow yourself to grow

Recreating old experiences by holding on to ideas about them can disconnect you from the present. So, to be fully present you will want to let go of those old ideas so that you can have that deeper awareness that contributes to personal expansion.

It might seem like a paradox that letting go of what you know is how you become most fully aware. However, realize that letting go does not mean that you disconnect from old experiences entirely. It just means that you let those experiences go into your collective awareness. Letting them go into your collective awareness is not something you do. It is actually something you allow. The process is natural and your job is to manage resistance to it.

How do you act each day with regard to outcomes or results? Since letting go sets the stage for your best ideas, it is a critical part of the cycle. In fact, it is often the most challenging part. Your ideas don't have to be monumental and your actions and results don't have to be earth shattering in order to live fully. But if you get stuck in a non-productive cycle by holding on to judgments, conclusions, positions, and similar outcome concepts, then your experience can be much less than fulfilling. Instead of engaging in things that are inspiring, you will spend your time resisting the creative nature of experience.

That's why it can be useful to be disciplined in order to let go of those outcome-oriented ideas. Just as rites of passage could be severe in primitive cultures, so today you will want to do whatever it takes to let go of those old cycles. How can you do that? Following are three things can help you.

First, you will be practicing both mental and physical clearing of experiential cycles by doing your daily routine. Meditation or relaxation that aims toward mindfulness and, physical exercise that simply moves the body to let go (a sort of "mindfulness of the body") can help support ongoing integration of experience.

These exercises provide subtle energy shifts intended to allow experience to integrate into your collective awareness. They can be very helpful in the short run and over longer time periods, they will have a profound effect on your ability to let go and integrate your experience. You might also want to plan periodic getaways designed to help you let go of specific experience so that all can integrate into your collective awareness. Years ago, Sundays served that purpose to some extent by being a day of rest. Today, you might want to plan similar days of rest or vacations that can serve that same purpose.

Second, you can surround yourself with people who are inspired and excited about their ideas. They will naturally encourage you to let go of unproductive experiential cycles. They will also share with you their inspired ideas, which then become part of your collective awareness. Being around people who are very judgmental won't help you let go and reconnect you're your own inspirational gravity.

Finally, if you can't seem to let go of those old judgments that continue to influence and keep you stuck in an old cycle, then you can get outside help much as people in primitive tribes did by engaging in their rites of passage. The tribal member making the passage from one stage of life to another was often helped by the whole tribe in dramatic ways to make the break. So, too, can you get that help when your own efforts are not enough.

A key to getting that outside help is an understanding of what you are doing. You are not a sick or broken human being. You are stuck, usually as the result of a useless belief. The job of those assisting you is to help you get unstuck. Once free, it will be your job to stay unstuck by assuming the responsibility for your own creative growth. In other words, once someone has helped you to recognize and let go of a useless belief, it will be your job to work with future resistance as it occurs. You, not your counselor or therapist, are the creator of your life.

Labeling yourself as having a medical/psychological problem is a conclusion or judgment. Holding on to that label is resistance and it can keep you right where you are. It is resistance to experiential cycles and it is a way to convince yourself that you have no influence in a particular matter, i.e. you are not to blame. It is like trying not to look at anything red. Letting go is less about letting go of something in the past and more about where you are going next. In other words, the way you let go is by taking hold of something new. You change your primary or cycle initiating idea. It is one thing to experience a cold. It is another to state, as some kind of truth, that you get a cold every time the seasons change. That belief isn't true, but it *is* creative. If you are stuck, get

154

someone to help you change your belief, not someone or something to help you shift the blame.

The Natural Experiential Cycle is natural and it can include the experience of sickness. The issue is your own resistance to the cycle and it can create mental, physical and spiritual challenges. Let go of the title or conclusion you created for yesterday's experience and look for your best idea for this day.

You can find a mental health professional to help you let go and make way for something new and inspiring. It is essential that he or she understand how to uncover and release old conclusions that need to move into your collective awareness where they can help as an integrated whole to provide inspirational ideas for today. Such an individual must support the completion of experiential cycles rather than just conceptual cycles. Shifting blame can end a conceptual cycle but it won't end an experiential cycle.

Many of these stuck cycles go back to childhood. A particular cycle of experience might have created such complex mental webs of thought that it is virtually impossible for you to break free of them without help from someone who is outside of your thinking process.

In addition, you can find a health practitioner who does "energy" work. That can include massage therapy, acupuncture, chiropractic, and other work designed to remove any physical blocks to the natural energy that flows through your body. Remember, you are just energy according to quantum physicists. It is much like the "physical mindfulness" that I described above. Blocks or resistance can occur both mentally in the form of beliefs and judgments and physically in the form of misaligned vertebrae, pinched nerves, and so forth.

As Deepak Chopra has said, "What is a cell, then? It is a memory that has built some matter around itself, forming a specific pattern." Sometimes it can be helpful to work directly at the physical level on cellular memory to release you from old patterns of belief and behavior.

Check out your health care provider carefully. Don't think that you can just turn yourself over to someone else in order to fix you. That would be denying your own creative nature and it is a way to avoid working with your own resistance.

You will want to be disciplined with your own thinking in order to complete experiential cycles that keep you in unproductive and uninspiring behavior. It is simply being disciplined in terms of letting go. This absolute letting go is not a rejection or denial of any past experience. On the contrary, it is actually an end to resisting it. The way you do that is by allowing that experience to become a part of the mix of experiences that constitute your life.

For those past experiences that were particularly traumatic, letting go can be very challenging because of the fear that it might happen again. Be disciplined by allowing the experience to integrate. Discipline is not physical or mental abuse. Physical or mental abuse does not help you let go of an old experiential cycle; instead, it helps the resistance to persist.

Identify your split second decision point

You can change your mind and your perspective in a split second. Consider the famous picture on the right (Fig. 7). What do you see? There are two ways to see this picture. If you see an old lady looking down and to your left, then look for the young lady by refocusing on the outline of the white face and neck looking toward the rear. If you see a

Figure 7

156

young lady, then change your focus by seeing the young girl's ear as the old woman's eye.

How long did it take you to change your focus? Once you were able to see the two faces, that change was instantaneous. That's how long it takes you to go from inspired thoughts to fear-based thoughts. You can begin to manifest your dream instantly by simply changing your focus.

Remember how resonance worked when I suggested in Chapter One that you not look at anything red? What you focus on reveals everything that resonates with that idea. So when you change your focus, you also change your perspective and see a completely different world. One world is the world associated with and resonating with your inspiring idea and the other world is the world associated with and resonating with whatever you fear.

That change in your world happens in the same instant that it takes to shift your perspective with a new idea. Here is another example (fig. 8) of a change in focus that results in a completely different experience.

Figure 8

Do you see a black chalice? Change your focus and see the two gray faces looking at each other. How long did it take? Also, ask yourself what thoughts came into your mind as you looked from one perspective and what thoughts came into your mind as you looked from the other perspective. What resonated with a chalice and what resonated with the faces? In the same way, a split second can change your whole world from fearful to inspired.

Become aware of your thoughts and of the moment you begin to feel resistance. This is the time when you can change your primary thoughts from those that resonate with what inspires you to those that resonate with what frightens you. By holding on to your inspired focus, you will begin to influence what is going on around you in a more positive way, even if those events feel very threatening.

Failure is not an option

Failure is actually not an option. Success is a natural occurrence. It is automatic. Your option is not whether you will be a success or a failure. Your option is whether you will be successful in creating experience that is expansive and uplifting or whether you will be successful in creating experience that is dull and lifeless. If you choose to create an expansive process, you will feel value and fulfillment regardless of how others define it. What you will feel is internal and no external events, rocks, boulders, or anything else can take that away.

Does death take that creative opportunity away? I don't know what death does or is. What I do know, however, is that ideas don't represent truth but they do create it. So, I choose to believe (creatively) that since I am energy at my core essence and since energy can be neither created nor destroyed, then the creative energy that is me remains after death. Whether I get to be reborn and go around this life again or I move to a higher spiritual level or I become Santa Claus is a mystery. I am very happy leaving it as such. I like and allow discovery (most of the time).

I do know that energy naturally manifests in a Natural Experiential Cycle and that manifestation is what I understand to be expanding awareness. So, I am going to believe (create) the idea that awareness will continue for me after death. You can believe/create whatever you choose.

158

Failure, however, is not an option. It is not an option because awareness is a gift that you have whether you engage it or you resist it. Meeting each event and experience from the perspective of optimal influence can help you stay grounded everyday. How can you influence what you encounter and how will you allow what you encounter to influence you? Making those decisions is how you work with resistance and engage in the creative process. Sometimes those events and experiences are pleasurable and sometimes painful. Although defining and labeling events and experiences is part of the Natural Cycle, those definitions are just that. They are part of the Cycle.

Awareness cannot fail although experience can hurt. I cannot *not* know what I know, including pain. I can, however, allow that knowing to integrate into collective awareness giving me an expanded capacity to experience my life. The hurt that I feel will go away if I allow it.

Summary

Grounding the life that inspires you requires ongoing vigilance. You will want to develop your observer skills, which will allow you to step outside of your current cycle (to a higher order of change) and observe what is going on for you at any particular time. You will want to observe in order to see the truth of the present. That truth is the outcome of your intention. It is what is in your life now and its value lies in revealing beliefs that lie at a subconscious level.

So, for example, you will want to be able to observe when you are feeling resistance. That means stepping outside of whatever it is that is bothering you and simply being aware that you are bothered in some way. Being able to do that will make it possible for you to identify which of the three resistance points is present for you. With that observation, you will know that a split second decision is ready to occur. Knowing this, you will be able to remind yourself to stay conscious of inspirational gravity (your core energetic desire) as opposed to an illusory goal that fear is creating. Staying conscious will help you make the choice that keeps you in your inspired game in a free and authentic way. Which perspective will you choose, fear or that which inspires you? Each will reveal and manifest a different reality.

Remember that success is natural and that it is not dictated by conceptual success but by experiential success. It is your own resistance to the path or cycle of experience that gets in the way and staying grounded everyday is simply being vigilant when in resistance. Being vigilant will help you avoid default perspectives that will keep you from expanding experience.

Have a routine that you use every day to help keep you conscious with regard to your own energy. If you miss a day or a week simply start again. Make it your anchor to help stay connected to your essence. Celebrate your learning in order to help allow and integrate all of your experience whether pleasurable or painful. Celebration isn't just for winning something and it isn't always fun and happy. It is for experience itself and the quantum leap that can occur as experience brings you personal expansion. Finally, be disciplined to be present. Allow the process of optimal influence rather than control to create your experiences.

Stop judging and predicting. Instead, start anticipating deeper and more profound experience even in the tiniest daily opportunity. Your life is what it is. The path of inspiration is what it is. Allow the experience of your life to be what it is. Let go of it so it can integrate and move on to what is present and possible for you now.

160

CONCLUSION

A hand moves, and the fire's whirling takes different
shapes:
All things change when we do.
The first word, "Ah," blossoms into all others.
Each of them is true.

"Singing Image of Fire"
Kukai

Each word you say or think is true. It is not true in the sense of being a fact. But it is true in terms of being the first appearance or effect of a Natural Experiential Cycle. It is like an incantation that begins the magic of your creation. Each word is your magic wand.

At the core of who you are is an energetic fire taking different shapes in the world. All energy is connected or more accurately, all energy supports the same fire. And as any part of that fire changes, so, too, does the whole fire change. You are not alone: rather, you are part of the mix of creative energy both influencing and being influenced.

You are energy. Stay connected to that energy by feeling it. When your energy is low, you can allow it to be low and let go until you feel renewed. When you find that your energy is low every day you can say, "I am energy" and allow that thought to reveal through resonance those ideas and things that feel energetic to you. You can allow that connected feeling to bring forward a new idea. The process is natural. You don't need a degree to know what inspires you. You do need to let go, however, and you do need to be conscious.

You ground the life that inspires you by making conscious choices in that split-second in time when resistance based on fear is tempting you to default to an old idea or perspective. Old ideas can be useful, but they can also be useless. The only way to know is to stay conscious and know the truth of what is currently in your life.

The discovery zone is not a comfortable place. This doesn't necessarily mean that it is a place of hard work or pain. It just means that it is a place of energy. You will tend to feel alive when you are in the discovery zone.

You can feel alive when you are climbing Mt. Everest and you can feel alive when you are going about your business at work or weeding the garden. The key is not *where* you are but *who* you are. The key is not overcoming resistance but working with it. The key is not being busy every day but being grounded every day.

The alchemists sought the elixir of life, which was that medicinal preparation that could prolong life or turn lead into gold. The good news is that you don't have to make such a preparation because it is a gift you already have. It is creative energy and you have an endless supply. You only need to recognize it. Be aware of what inspires you and you have connected to your gift of life. What inspires you also energizes and breathes life into your life experience.

I come from a line of energetic people. They include inventors, writers, kings, business developers, and much more. So do you. While our ancestors are defined in different ways, they were all energetic people with inspired ideas simply because of who they were: creative beings. At what times and places did those energetic people know who they were and act on it? At what times and places did those people forget who they were and default to an old idea based on fear? What part of their energy has passed to you and what old judgments and beliefs of theirs are you holding on to? Which ones are useful and which ones are useless? The source of energy and beliefs that run your life can come from far in the past. Remember that it only takes an instant for you to disconnect from useless ideas and beliefs and connect to the energy that is you.

We live in an abundant universe. There are billions of stars and leaves and kernels of corn. There is an abundance of people and places. Some people say that God or the Great Spirit or a similar intelligence made this abundant universe. If that is true, then one way to connect with that Spirit of spirits is to share in the abundance. In fact, one could ask whether anyone can claim to be connected to that Spirit of spirits if he or she is not experiencing abundance in their life. That abundance could look like money or friends or living with nature or something else where the proverbial cup is overflowing. In each case, material abundance is just the physical manifestation of an abundance of experience.

We have a legacy together. We are all part of the same fire of creative energy no matter that we appear as different. Remember, however, we each make our own choices from either fear or inspiration; and in so doing, we all influence the fire. Those choices manifest naturally creating expanding experience or contracting experience. Allow your choices to represent what inspires you and you will be an expansive part of the fire we all share.

Grounding the life that inspires you takes engagement, courage, and vigilance. None of those characteristics require degrees or talent or good looks. What is required is a willingness to change. Inspiration is a gift. You open that gift by engaging in your best ideas. Having the courage to do that while remaining vigilant to resistance will change you and others. That change will be an expanding capacity for experience and it will make the fire we all share burn brighter.

NOTES

[1] Margaret Wheatley, *Leadership and the New Science* (San Francisco: Berrett-Koehler Publishers), 112.

[2] Jon Krakauer, *Into Thin Air: A Personal Account of the Mount Everest Disaster* (New York: Villard).

[3] Robert G. Jahn and Brenda J. Dunne, *Margins of Reality, The Role of Consciousness in the Physical World* (New York: Harcourt Brace Javanovich), 201.

[4] Qtd. in Jahn and Dunne, 324.

[5] Ibid., 255.

[6] Wheatley, 95.

[7] Ibid, 95.

[8] Joseph Campbell, *The Hero with a Thousand Faces* (Princeton: Princeton University Press), 10.

[9] Timothy Ferris, *Coming of Age in the Milky Way* (New York: William Morrow and Company), 288.

[10] Ferris, 286.

[11] Ven. Henepola Gunaratan, "Mindfulness In Plain English," http://www.budsas.org/ebud/mfneng/mind0.htm.

[12] Qtd. from Center for Mindfulness in Medicine, Health Care, and Society brochure (Worcester, MA).

[13] Wheatley, 118.

[14] Campbell, 59-60.

[15] William James, *The Letters of William James: Bartlett's Familiar Quotations* (Boston: Little, Brown and Company, 2002), 581.

[16] Joe Hyams, *Zen in the Martial Arts* (Los Angeles: J. P. Tarcher), 19.

[17] Stephen Mitchell, *The Enlightened Heart, An Anthology of Sacred Poetry* (New York: Harper Perennial), 95.

[18] Qtd. in Campbell, 238-239.

[19] Jackson, Susan A. and Csikszentmihalyi, Mihaly, *Flow in Sports, The keys to optimal experiences and performances* (Champaign, IL: Human Kinectics), 5.

BIBLIOGRAPHY

Campbell, Joseph. *The Hero with a Thousand Faces*. Princeton, NJ: Princeton University Press, 1973.

Chopra, Deepak. *How to Know God, The Soul's Journey into the Mystery of Mysteries*. New York, NY: Harmony Books, 2000.

Dyer, Wayne. *The Power of Intention*. Carlsbad, CA: Hay House, 2004.

Ferris, Timothy. *Coming of Age in the Milky Way*. New York, NY: William Morrow and Company, 1988.

Gawain, Shakti. *Creative Visualization*. Novato, CA: Nataraj Publishing, 2002.

Hyams, Joe. *Zen in the Martial Arts*. Los Angeles: J.P. Tarcher, 1979.

Jahn, Robert G. and Dunne, Brenda J. *Margins of Reality: The Role of Consciousness in the Physical World*. New York: Harcourt Brace Javanovich, 1987.

Krakauer, Jon. *Into Thin Air: A Personal Account of the Mount Everest Disaster*. New York: Villard, 1997.

Mitchell, Stephen. *The Enlightened Heart, An Anthology of Sacred Poetry*. New York: HarperPerennial, 1993.

Tolle, Eckhart. *The Power of Now*. Novato, CA: New World Library, 1999.

Wheatley, Margaret. *Leadership and the New Science*. San Francisco: Berrett-Koehler Publishers, 1999.

Contact information

SERVICES AVAILABLE

Ted Case loves speaking to conventions, and business and professional organizations on his powerful success strategies for group and individual empowerment. In addition, Ted teaches these strategies bring clarity and focus to individuals and teams in retreat settings and project planning meetings.

Learn to: revitalize the passion of your business; overcome limiting resistance to your business or personal achievements; and develop a daily practice to insure consistent success. Learn to unleash the power blocked by your resistance and step into the flow of being moved.

After working with Ted, you will accelerate growth of your business; reach those goals that seemed unreachable; and create a powerfully integrated team environment. These results can be utilized to turn ideas into money and ROI.

To sign up for Ted's monthly tips on how to connect with the energy of success, visit his website at
www.inspirationalgravity.com.

For information on Ted's programs and availability, contact:

ted@casedynamics.com
or call: 1-303-898-0423

Praise for Ted Case

"Ted did an incredible job of tailoring the seminar to the audience. We need more in-services like this!"
Teresa Schmid, RN
Swedish Medical Center

"You've helped me develop more of a focus for my business. I wish I had hired you when I first started, as it would have saved me thousands of dollars."
Beth Anderson, President
Cottonwood Connection, Inc.

"I really appreciate your professionalism and dedication... The staff commented on the excellent program you gave and the interest and attention the attendees had."
Toni Freeman
Jefferson County Libraries

"I feel you see the sign of a great program when people don't want to leave. Our people stayed over an hour. I would definitely have this speaker back!!"
Michael Akers, Speaker Committee Chair
Mile Hi Church, Business Honoring Spirituality

"Exceptionally knowledgeable and passionate about helping others achieve success. Ted's style is genuine and he creates a brilliant learning environment of solid content and inspiration."
Jami Jackson, Class Participant
Colorado Free University